HAVE FUN at HOME

WRITTEN BY ALISON MALONEY
AND CHRIS STEVENS

ILLUSTRATED BY KAREN DONNELLY,
A. J. GARCES AND DAVID WOODROFFE

EDITED BY SALLY PILKINGTON AND RACHEL CARTER
AND ADAPTED BY LAUREN FARNSWORTH
AND JONNY LEIGHTON

DESIGNED BY ZOE BRADLEY

COVER DESIGNED BY JOHN BIGWOOD

Contents

Introduction

Whether your family is staying indoors for the day because it's a bit miserable outside, or you're hanging out in the garden or yard instead of going to the park, this book will make sure you have loads of fun at home.

There are lots of cool and creative ways to get everyone in your family spending time together, and no end to the fun things to do.

Have Fun At Home is packed with activities for both children and adults to enjoy. Some are practical, some are arty, some are a little bit silly – but they are all guaranteed to be great fun.

Whether you have ten minutes or a whole day, this book has a perfect pastime for you. Simple instructions mean you can turn your hand to arts and crafts, games, recipes, magic tricks and much, much more.

Dotted throughout the book, you'll come across these hand symbols:

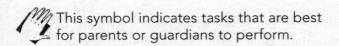 This symbol indicates tasks that are best for parents or guardians to perform.

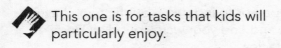 This one is for tasks that kids will particularly enjoy.

So, if you're not going out, why not dive in to this book and start having fun at home right away.

Create A Crazy Golf Course

Guess what? Your home is a crazy golf green just waiting to happen and this is one course where you're guaranteed free membership!

All the materials you'll need to build the course are within arms' reach. The aim of the game is to knock the ball into a saucepan or frying pan – but first you have to hit tricky targets and find your way around all kinds of challenging obstacles.

Half the fun of this game is designing the course and steering clear of its traps.

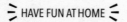

You will need:

- a long umbrella, a walking stick or a hockey stick to use as your golf club • saucepans and/or frying pans
- lots of obstacles, such as books and tin cans
- a tennis ball

- - - - - - - - - - - - - - - - -

SAFE-TEE TIPS

Before you 'tee off', hide anything breakable. It is a good idea to use a tennis ball instead of a real golf ball, and to stay right away from rooms with expensive, fragile objects, such as televisions and laptops. When you are playing, remember to tap the ball lightly – it will help to make your stroke much more accurate.

A COURSE IN DESIGN

Now you're ready to set up a series of challenging holes. Use a combination of objects such as tin cans, books, shoes and rows of toy cars, or try building these holes:

The Box Challenge: Zigzag between old DVD or video games boxes balanced on their sides, but don't knock any over!

The Bath Bunker: The bathroom course starts in the bath – now renamed 'the bunker'. Instead of trying to play your way out of the bath by hitting the ball straight up the side, try aiming for the end opposite the taps.

Tin Can Alley: Tin cans make great building blocks for bridges and tunnels. Before the ball lands in a hole, hit it through a series of tin can bridges in the right order.

Hole too soon, and you'll have to go back to the start and begin the course again.

Roll Up, Roll Up: The ball must travel through a triangular tunnel of books, then bounce off a marked spot on the skirting board, roll down an avenue of toy cars, slip between two shoes without touching them, and roll up another book into a saucepan.

You don't need to build *all* your holes. Why not put one under a bed? If you have stairs make them a central part of your course. Tell players they must hit the ball down the stairs and into an awaiting saucepan.

Old lengths of guttering are great for hitting the ball onto chairs or around tight corners.

MARVELLOUS MARBLE GOLF

If space is tight, try playing desktop crazy golf using a marble as a ball. Hit it with a pencil through a maze of books, tins and toys, or flick it with a fingertip along a path of rulers and cardboard tubes.

WHAT'S THE SCORE?

However you play, keep count of the number of times each player hits the ball before finishing the course. Add five penalty points to this score whenever obstacles are missed out or knocked down.

Once all the players have completed the course, the player with the lowest score wins.

Tricky Twist: Once in a game, each player can insist that their opponent wears a blindfold for a crucial shot.

Start Your Own Slime Factory

Imagine being able to make as much slime as you want. Doesn't that just sound amazing? Finally you will be able to throw out all of the old stuff that is covered in dust and carpet fluff. Making your own slime is lots of fun, and it means you'll never run out of it ever again. (Your parents will be thrilled!)

You will need:

- 3 tbsp borax powder (available online or in supermarkets near the detergents)
- water • 5 tbsp PVA glue
- 1 tsp food colouring

Mix the borax powder with 275 ml of water in a measuring jug. Stir the mixture until the borax has dissolved and then put it to one side.

In another bowl, mix together the PVA glue, five tablespoons of water and the food colouring. Stir until the mixture has completely combined and is an even colour throughout.

Now, this is when the magic happens. Very carefully, pour a little of the borax solution into the glue mixture and stir – the slime should immediately thicken. Continue to add the borax mixture a little bit at time, stirring until you end up with a thick, gloopy mixture that you can handle and squash together in your hands.

If your slime still leaves a gluey residue on your hands, hold it under the tap for a few seconds to rinse it off. Now you have your very own batch of slime to do with what you will.

Top tip: Make your slime last longer by keeping it in an airtight container.

Warning: Slime feels great and is fun to play with, but it is not safe to eat and can be very difficult to get out of hair. Keep out of reach of younger children.

Play Indoor Fishing

With this game, you can go on a fishing trip come rain or shine. Just don't try eating these flappy friends for supper.

For two people fishing you will need:

• 2 magnets • 2 sticks
• 2 pieces of string at least 1 m long
• a plain, medium-sized cardboard box or something with a similar shape and size • sheets of white card • sticky tape
• scissors • a box of paperclips • pens or paints

To make a fishy template, draw a fish 15 cm long on a piece of card. Cut it out. Then make as many fish as you want by placing the template on another sheet of card, drawing around it and cutting out your catch.

 Have a competition to see who can decorate their fish the best.

Now take the box and paint waves and seaweed around the outside. Or, draw your designs on some A4 paper and attach them to the outside of your container using sticky tape.

Write a number between five and ten on every fish. Then slide a paperclip over the nose of each one. Throw your shoal into the box.

To make the fishing rods, tie lengths of string to the ends of the sticks, then tie a magnet to the end of each piece of string.

See who can score the most points by dangling their magnet in the pond and taking it in turns to catch a fish by its paperclip.

Delicious Chocolate Chip Muffins

These delicious treats are perfect to make for parties, picnics or presents, or just because they taste great. Eat them warm, not long after they have come out of the oven, when the chocolate chips are still melted and gooey, or if you can manage to resist them, store in an airtight container for another day.

You will need:

- 250 g (9 oz) self-raising flour
- ½ tsp salt • 100 g (4 oz) sugar
- 200 ml milk • one egg
- 85 g (3 oz) butter or margarine
- 85 g (3 oz) chocolate chips
- 12 paper cases

- - - - - - - - - - - - - - - - - - - -

 Melt the butter (either in a microwave or in a bowl placed in hot water). Mix the butter, milk and egg in a large bowl.

In a separate bowl, combine the flour, salt and sugar. Make a well in the centre with a wooden spoon, and pour the wet liquid into it, mixing together well. Add the chocolate chips and stir until the whole mixture begins to come together.

 Spoon the mixture into the paper cases placed either in a muffin tin or on a baking tray. Fill each to about halfway. This mixture should fill a dozen cases.

 Place the muffins in an oven and bake at gas mark 6/200°C/400°F for 20 minutes or until they have risen and are a lovely golden colour.

Leave the muffins to stand for a few minutes and then remove them from the tin and cool on a wire rack.

Make An Artificial Eye

Why not make an artificial eye to look at the world in a whole new way? It's amazing what you can make with an empty cardboard tube!

You will need:

• a cardboard tube (the cylindrical kind with a plastic lid that you find on potato snacks packets – remember to clean out the crumbs!)
• a ruler • a drawing pin • a craft knife • masking tape
• a felt-tip pen • a sheet of tracing paper • kitchen foil

- - - - - - - - - - - - - - - - - - -

With a felt-tip pen draw a straight line around the tube about 5 cm from the closed base.

 Using a sharp craft knife or scissors, ask an adult to carefully cut the tube into two pieces along the line you have drawn.

With a drawing pin, poke a hole through the centre of the metal base of the tube.

Cut a circle of tracing paper that fits snugly inside the plastic lid of the tube. This will act as the screen of your 'eye'. Secure it with some tape.

Put the plastic lid (with the screen inside) back on to your tube – on the open end of the short piece of tube.

Next, put the long tube back on the other side of the lid, and tape it in place with masking tape.

To prevent light from leaking into the tube, roll it in a double layer of kitchen foil and tape the foil tightly into place.

You should now have something that looks a little bit like a kitchen foil telescope. This is your artificial eye.

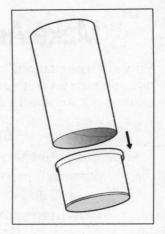

On a bright sunny day, look outside and find an object that won't move – such as a tree or building. Hold the open end of your tube to one eye. Press it firmly against your face to cut out as much light as possible.

You should be able to see a colour image that has been projected through the pin hole onto the screen. It will be an upside-down image.

Top tip: If you can't see the image clearly, try putting a blanket over your head and poking the tube out of a gap in the material. This will reduce the amount of light that can leak into the end of the tube that is in front of your eye.

Make Your Own Place Mat

Brighten up mealtimes with a personalized place mat of your own unique design. Make it a family collage or a work of art, an explosion of colour or a stylish piece of interior design. Whatever you choose, it beats boring shop-bought place mats any day. Why not make a set for the whole family. It'll give everyone something colourful to look at while waiting for their meal. Here are two methods of creating a mat masterpiece.

THE ARTISTIC METHOD
You will need:

- a sheet of paper (A4) • a sheet of corrugated card (A4)
- paint, crayons or felt-tip pens • a glue stick
- sticky back plastic

— — — — — — — — — — — — — — — — — —

Get creative. You are now a designer of exclusive place mats. Draw a picture, a pattern or a series of shapes on your paper – you could even draw your favourite meal.

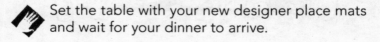 When the design is done glue it to the sheet of card and then cover both sides with the sticky back plastic, being careful to smooth it out (as instructed on the packaging) so no bubbles are trapped.

Set the table with your new designer place mats and wait for your dinner to arrive.

THE COLLAGE METHOD
You will need:

- a sheet of paper (A4) • a sheet of corrugated card (A4)
- collage materials e.g. photos, magazine pictures,
foil wrapping paper, stickers, stars, etc.
- pens • a glue stick • sticky back plastic

Choose the pictures you want for the place mat. Family photos look much nicer if they are cut in irregular shapes, rather than square. Glue the pictures to the paper and decorate around them with your other collage materials. Personalize your mat further by writing your name in bold letters.

When the design is done, glue it to the sheet of card and cover both sides with sticky back plastic. Alternatively, pop to a local shop that can laminate it for you.

Catch A Shadow

Believe it or not, it really is possible to catch someone's shadow. Here's how ...

You will need:

- large sheets of white paper (at least A2)
- a torch • black paper • a pencil
- a glue stick • sticky tack • sticky tape • scissors

Use the sticky tack to attach a large piece of white paper to a wall. One person stands sideways to the wall about 60 cm away from the paper. This person is the 'sitter' whose shadow will be caught.

Pull the curtains together to darken the room and shine the torch onto the sitter's profile. Experiment with the distance between the light and the sitter until you get a sharp shadow of their profile that fits on the sheet of paper. The closer you move the torch to the sitter, the larger the shadow or 'silhouette' will be.

Draw around the outline of the silhouette with a pencil. Then take down the paper and cut out the profile.

Tape the paper profile to a sheet of black paper. Using the white cut-out as a template, snip around it again so that the profile is cut out in black paper, too.

Finally, use the glue stick to mount the black cut-out onto a new sheet of white paper. Write your sitter's name and the date at the bottom of the paper.

FREESTYLE SILHOUETTE

In Victorian times, there was a craze for pictures like these. People became skilled at cutting tiny portraits out of paper without even drawing them first. Why not have a go at cutting a profile of someone's face from a black sheet of paper without drawing the outline? It's more tricky than it sounds.

Did you know?
The silhouette was named after French politician Etienne de Silhouette, who died in 1767. He was a mean, tight-fisted man and people joked he wouldn't waste his money on a painted portrait when he could have a paper cut-out instead.

Make A Piñata Pig

A piñata is a colourful papier-mâché figure, filled with sweets. It's usually hung from a tree where children can take turns to hit it until the sweets tumble out. It's a brilliant idea for children's celebrations.

Although many people associate the tradition with Mexico, it actually began as a Chinese custom, and was introduced to the West by the explorer Marco Polo.

You need to allow time for drying, so start making your piñata about a week before you throw your party.

You will need:

- a balloon • 1 ¼ l water • 40 g plain flour
- newspapers • 5 paper cups, cut in half
- sticky tape • paper for ears
- pink poster paint and brush
- black marker pen • individually wrapped sweets
- strong string (about 2 m)
- a stick for hitting

— — — — — — — — — — — — — — —

Blow up a balloon as large as possible, to make the body of the pig. Tape the bottom halves of four of the paper cups onto the body for legs and one to the pointed end of the balloon for the pig's snout.

To make the glue, mix the flour with 225 ml of the water. In a pan, boil 900 ml of water and then stir in the flour mixture. Simmer for two minutes and leave to cool before pouring into a large container.

Tear the newspaper into strips and dunk them one at a time into your glue mix. Run the strip between two fingers to remove extra glue. Smooth the gluey paper over the pig, overlapping them slightly until everything is completely covered.

Allow this layer to dry before starting another. Aim for three to six layers depending on how easily you'd like the piñata to break.

When it's dry, cut a flap in the back. Burst and remove the balloon and fill the pig with sweets before taping the flap shut.

Paint the pig pink. Cut two ear-shaped pieces out of paper and paint. Then glue them on to the head and draw on the pig's features.

Finally, tie the string around the pig's tummy, then loop the ends over a branch or any convenient spot. Make sure the pig hangs low enough for even the smallest visitor to your party to reach.

Everyone should take turns whacking the piñata until it breaks, spilling its contents. You could offer a prize to the piñata champion, but it's probably best to share out the sweets between all contestants.

Have A Keepie-Uppie Competition

If you want to look like superstar players Cristiano Ronaldo, Lionel Messi or Megan Rapinoe, you need to master the 'keepie-uppie'.

Stand on one leg with your other foot raised, the toes higher than the heel. Drop the ball onto the flat top of your foot as you flick your toes up lightly. You are aiming to bounce the ball just a few centimetres. The trick is to make sure the ball doesn't fly forwards – if it does, you'll be lunging clumsily after it. Keep it bouncing up and spinning slightly back, towards your shin. You can even add the odd knee bounce now and again.

When you've mastered the keepie-uppie, have a competition with someone to see who can do the most in one minute. Or, face each other and do keepie-uppies until one person drops their ball.

EXPERT SKILLS

Try switching feet between kicks, or letting the ball bounce off your chest. The ultimate trick is to tip your head back and launch the ball up onto your forehead – balance it there for a few seconds then let it roll back down onto your foot.

Create A Moving Easter Card

Pop-up cards are lots of fun and with this one the little chick opens and shuts its beak as if it is really tweeting! They are brilliant for Easter, but you can make them at any time of the year and with any animal – or person – you can think of. Why not try making a robin at Christmas, or your favourite pet?

You will need:

- 2 pieces of thin card in different colours
- glue • scissors
- colouring pens, pencils or crayons

- -

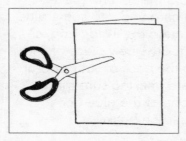

Fold one piece of card in half. Cut a line of about 5 cm across the middle of the crease.

Fold back each of the flaps to make two triangles, leaving a triangular hole at the crease. Sharpen the folds by running a fingernail along the folded edge of each triangle.

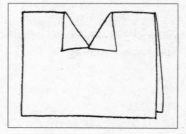

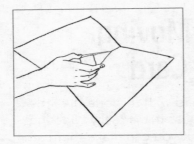

Unfold the triangles and open the card to about halfway.

Push one of the triangles through the hole and pinch to make it stand up. Repeat with the other triangle.

Close the card and press down on the folds to strengthen the creases. The 'beak' should now pop up when you open the card.

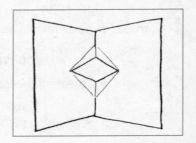

Fold the second piece of card and dab some glue around the inside edges. Stick the new piece of card to the back of your pop-up card, making sure that none of the glue goes near the beak.

Now draw your bird around the beak and write your seasonal message.

How To Play Achi

This game, which originated in West Africa, is ideal for two people to enjoy. It is perfect to play on the beach or in a sandpit, but you can adapt it to play almost anywhere – including drawing it out on a piece of paper.

Mark out lines to form a square board as shown below. Find something to use as counters, for example, pebbles and shells, or coins and buttons.

HOW TO PLAY

One person plays using pebbles, the other with shells.

Toss a coin to decide which player starts. Then, taking it in turns, place your counters on the 'board' at any of the points where lines intersect. When all eight counters are in position, players take turns to move their counters into the single empty spot, aiming to be the first player to get three counters in a row.

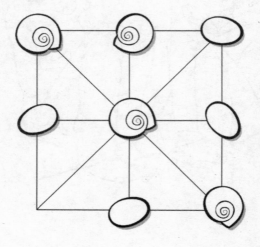

Twenty Questions

In this game one player thinks of an animal, plant or object and the other players must try and guess what it is by asking a maximum of twenty questions.

Each question can only be answered with a *'yes'* or a *'no'*. For example, you must not ask *'How many legs does it have?'* but you may ask *'Does it have four legs?'*

If the correct answer is guessed within the alloted number of questions the person who guesses wins the round and it is their turn to think of something.

Invent A Secret Handshake

Everyone knows the importance of a firm handshake – not a limp touch of the fingers, but a confident grip, matched with a smile. Secret handshakes are much cooler and can be really out-there – elbows, shoulders and even feet can be involved.

Try these moves, then put some together in a cool combination to make your own family handshake.

- Hook your fingertips together.

- Raise your hands so they are facing the other person and slap each other's palms in a 'high ten'.

- Hold out both hands palms facing upwards to be slapped.

- Wrap both hands around the other person's fist.

- Bump opposite elbows with each other twice.

- Bump opposite shoulders with each other three times.

- Hold your hands together, as if you're praying, then touch your middle fingers to your friend's middle fingers.

- Take it in turns to slap the back of the other person's right hand lightly.

- Link arms and hop around in a circle.

- Jump towards each other and bounce your chests together. (Don't attempt this with your parent if they have a big belly!)

SHAKE HANDS STREET STYLE

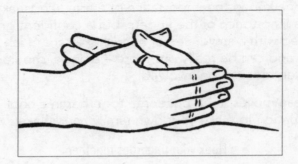

1. Start with an ordinary handshake.

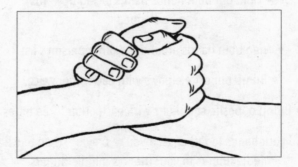

2. Drop your wrist so that your hands twist to a 90-degree angle and hook your thumbs together.

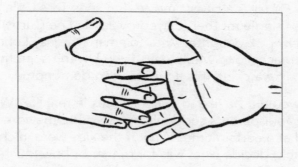

3. Slide your hands apart, wiggling your fingers to tickle each other's palm.

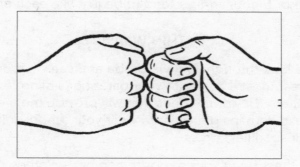

4. Bunch your hand into a fist and rap into the top of the other person's fist twice. Let their fist bounce twice on yours. Then lightly punch your knuckles together.

Have A Freaky Friday

Freaky Friday is a classic movie that sees Tess Coleman, a stylish single mother (played by Jamie Lee Curtis) and her rock chick daughter Ana Coleman (Lindsay Lohan) switch places for a whole day. If you haven't seen this film, then watching it is a fun thing to do at home.

What would it be like to switch places in real life? What if one of your parents suddenly had to do homework or go to bed at a certain time? What if the kids were in charge, and could decide what was for dinner or how much time on their tablets they were allowed?

Have your own Freaky Friday, Thursday, Sunday or any other day and find out. You could even try it out with a sibling or friend, and pretend to be just like each other!

THE SWAP

Take a look through your wardrobe and see what outfits you wear most – then, get your parent or sibling to wear them. Go for the ones that will provide the most contrast. Perhaps get them to wear your school uniform or your sparkliest dress.

Then, dress up in your opposite number's clothes. Maybe wear your parent's work uniform, or your big brother' or sister's sports outfit.

THE GAME

There are no rules for this game apart from acting like each other. Let your imaginations run riot. Your parents may not want to do homework when they're told to and may go and switch on the TV. Kids may want the family to have ice cream for dinner.

Make sure you remember to swap back again before you go outside, or you could get some very strange looks.

Make A Tiny Parachute

Make a toy parachute and watch it float to earth. All you need is a circle of cotton fabric 30 cm in diameter and eight pieces of thick thread each about 35 cm long.

Pinch the fabric at a point along the edge of the circle. Tie the end of a length of thread around the gather and knot the string. Tie the dangling end to a small, lightweight toy, such a plastic soldier. Repeat this for each piece of thread at regular intervals around the fabric.

In the garden, or wherever you have space indoors, pinch the centre of the fabric circle and pull it into a thin cone, swing the toy round, then let go, sending it high into the air. As the toy falls, the parachute will open.

Experiment to discover the lowest height that allows the chute to open successfully. Does it work from the bottom of the stairs or when you stand on a chair?

Why not make a parachute for each member of your family and see whose stays in the air longest?

Have A Finger Kickabout

You don't need a stadium that seats 80,000 people and a billionaire owner to play the 'beautiful game'. A kitchen table, a ping-pong ball and your fingers will do just fine.

Use a piece of chalk to mark out your pitch on a large, flat surface.

Place two open cardboard boxes on their sides to be your goals, or use egg cups for goal posts.

Use your forefinger and middle finger to 'run' across the table and to dribble the ball. You could make boots like the ones shown above with cardboard and papier-mâché, but bare fingers work just as well.

Make sure each team has an equal number of players. Two players can have an excellent match and can play

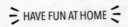

using their left and right hands – one hand playing an attack position, the other staying in defence. This takes practice and it helps if the pitch isn't too large.

THE RULES

• Keep one of your fingers in contact with the ground at all times. Superhuman leaps and 'flying' players are not allowed.

• Take a kick-off from the middle of the table after every goal.

• Corners and penalties are handled in the same way as in a full-sized game. If you grab your opponent's fingers, push or hold them away from the ball, that's a foul and your opponent gets a free kick.

• Your opponent gets a penalty flick if a foul occurs in the goal area.

• Five fouls add up to a yellow card, and two yellow cards mean a sending-off. A sending-off means a player can only use one hand.

• Holding the ball between your fingers, cupping the ball under your palm and using your thumb are all handball offences. Putting one finger on the ball to hold it in place before kicking it away is, however, fair play.

Sew Much Fun

Learning to sew is a great activity to be enjoyed together and means that you will be able to do any number of brilliant, crafty projects. It also means you will never be caught short with a hole in your socks again.

RUNNING STITCH

Running stitch is the most basic of stitches and is used for sewing fabric together. If you master this stitch you can sew almost anything. To secure your stitches, begin and end your sewing with a couple of stitches on top of each other.

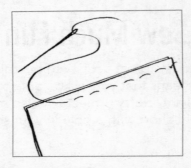

Push a threaded needle through the front side of the fabric. Then push it through from the back, leaving a couple of millimetres' gap. Continue. On each side of the fabric there should be stitches of even length, each separated by the same length of space. For heavier fabrics, stitches should be shorter, and for light fabrics the stitches can be slightly longer.

BACKSTITCH

Backstitch is the strongest sewing technique and will look like a continuous line of stitches, rather like the ones you would get from a sewing machine.

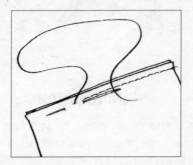

Secure your thread and then do the first stitch as you would for running stitch. As the needle pushes through to the front of the fabric, instead of going forward, bring the needle back to the end of the previous stitch and push through again. Then bring the needle through at the same distance in front of the finished stitch, pulling it back to stitch over the space once more.

HEMSTITCH

This is a clever stitch that you can't see from the front of the fabric. It is great for sewing hems and cuffs.

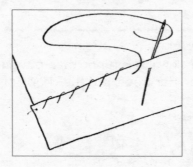

Secure your thread as before, this time sewing your stitches on the spot in the hem and not through the main part of the fabric. Working from right to left, pass the needle through the hem and pick up some strands at the back of the main fabric, just above the hem's edge. Take care not to push the needle all the way through otherwise the stitching will show, then pass the needle back through the hem. Repeat by picking up a few strands of the main fabric with your needle as before.

Create A Modern Masterpiece

BEAUTIFUL BLOW PICTURES

Blow painting makes really interesting pictures. It is particularly good for creating tree scenes.

You will need:

• paper • drinking straws • runny, water-based paint

- -

Dilute the paint until it is runny then put a few drops onto the paper. For trees, put the drops of paint at the

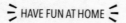

bottom of the page. Using the straw, blow the paint until you have achieved a pattern you like.

Turn the paper around and repeat with a different colour. Whatever you do, remember you have to blow, not suck. Keep going with more colours, until the picture is complete, and then leave to dry.

PAINTING WITH MARBLES

Paint-covered marbles will make great patterns on a plain sheet of paper, but be warned, it can get messy.

You will need:

- a washing up bowl or deep tray
- different coloured craft paints in small pots
- white paper • a few marbles • plastic spoons

Cut the paper to fit into the base of the bowl or tray and place it at the bottom.

Coat a marble with paint by dropping it into one of the paint-filled containers. Lift it out using a spoon and drop it onto the paper. Tilt the bowl or tray in different directions so the marble leaves a colourful trail.

Repeat with different coloured paints until you have a pattern all over the paper. When the picture is finished remove from the bowl and leave to dry.

Create A Magical Work Of Art

It's time for your parents to use their artistic talents for fun, instead of just painting the kitchen ceiling. Here's how to create a mesmerizing picture using crayons and black paint.

You will need:

- sheets of thick paper that won't tear easily – the bigger the better
- a pack of wax crayons
- black poster paint and a broad paintbrush
- newspaper • an old fork

- - - - - - - - - - - - - - - - - - - -

Using different crayons, decorate a sheet of paper with swirling patterns. Fill every centimetre with whirls and squiggles. Press down hard, and go back over your design. Take a long, loving look at your stunning masterpiece before you cover it up.

Put the sheet on a newspaper and brush black poster paint over it. Brush it on generously, so there isn't a glimpse of the patterns left.

Now leave the paint to dry.

Test the paint with your fingertip – the effect will be ruined if you start working when it is still wet.

When you are sure it is dry, take the fork and scrape its prongs against the black paint. It should reveal rainbow-like patterns underneath. Perhaps try to create one of these spectacular pieces of art:

- magical tigers at midnight

- jewels in an underground cavern

- planets in a distant galaxy

- explorers in their rainbow space rockets

- parrots in the deepest jungle (use dark green poster paint instead of black)

How To Customize A T-Shirt

Calling all skaters and DIY fashionistas – if you have an old white T-shirt that you never wear, here are two great ways to give it a new, seriously cool, lease of life.

TIE-DYE

A tie-dyed T-shirt is eye-catching but simple to achieve.

You will need:

- a white or light-coloured cotton T-shirt or top
- a bowl (bear in mind you won't be able to use it for food again) • rubber bands or pieces of string
- rubber gloves • a bucket
- cold-water dye and cold dye fix
- an old towel or tea towel
- an old wooden spoon or wooden washing tongs
- cold water • hot water • 6 tbsp salt

- - - - - - - - - - - - - - - - - - - -

Plan your design. For example, do you want small patterns in one area, or large circles all over? You can even have stripes. Look at the different designs you can create on the following pages.

Dampen the T-shirt by submerging it in water, then squeeze out the excess. If it is a new top, wash it first.

To create tie-dye circles, gather large or small bunches of fabric and twist rubber bands or tie the pieces of string tightly around the bottom of each bunch.

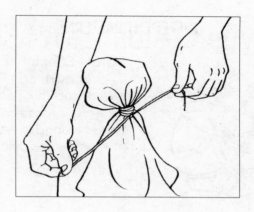

Put the bucket in the sink or bath and pour in two litres of cold water. Pour half a litre of hot water into a bowl and mix in the dye. Pour the dye mixture into the bucket and wash the bowl. Pour another half a litre of hot water into the bowl and mix it with the dye fix and the salt. Stir until all of the salt has dissolved and then pour the mixture into the bucket. Wearing rubber gloves, submerge the T-shirt into the diluted dye and stir slowly with the spoon or tongs for ten minutes. Poke the cloth to keep it submerged.

Leave the T-shirt in the bucket for an hour, stirring occasionally. Take out and rinse under cold water until the water runs clear.

Squeeze the shirt and then roll it in the towel or tea towel to remove excess water. Now take off the bands and marvel at the cool tie-dye effect.

Top tip: You may be eager to try out your new look but you have to wash and dry the T-shirt first. You don't want to end up with green skin!

DIFFERENT PATTERNS

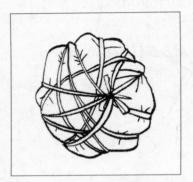

Marble Effect. For an all-over marbled effect, scrunch up the T-shirt and tie string or fasten rubber bands around it in a random fashion before dying.

Concentric Circles. For concentric circles (circles within circles) pinch a spot of fabric and then use several rubber bands spaced at regular intervals along the length of the fabric. You can do one big 'bull's-eye' pattern or a few smaller ones by using as many bands as you like.

Sunburst. Use marbles to create a different effect. For a sunburst pattern, wrap some material around a marble and then fix several rubber bands around the bunched fabric below, a centimetre or so apart.

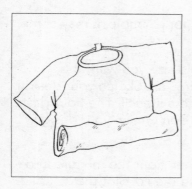

Stripes. For stripes, roll your T-shirt from top to bottom like a sausage as shown. Then place the rubber bands at intervals along the material.

BATIK T-SHIRT

Batik is thought to date back more than 2,000 years, but its exact origins are unknown. Batik is most common in Java and Bali, in Indonesia, where it was once the mark of wealth, position and even royalty.

Traditionally, designs are achieved with the use of hot wax, but to keep creative fingers from burning, here is a safer alternative. However, you will need patience – and a few days to spare.

You will need:

- white or light-coloured cotton T-shirt
- 75 g (2¾ oz) flour • 115 ml water
- 1 sheet of thick paper • cold-water dye • a paintbrush
- an old washing-up liquid or squeezy bottle
- 1 sheet of cardboard (the side of a cereal box will do)

First plan your design. Try it on rough paper first, colouring it in to see what the T-shirt will look like. Remember to think about colour – if you are painting red dye on to a yellow T-shirt, for example, it may come out orange.

Cut the paper to the shape and size you want the design to be (e.g. square or circular). Sketch your design on to the paper, then cut it into a stencil. The flour paste needs to go into the holes so don't make your design too fiddly or it will be difficult to cut out.

Mix the flour and water together. Pour the mixture into the squeezy bottle and replace the lid. Slot the cardboard between the front and back of the T-shirt to protect the fabric behind your design.

Lay the stencil on to the front of the T-shirt and carefully squeeze the flour paste into the holes. The areas covered in glue will be the ones that stay the same colour as the T-shirt. Now squeeze the paste around the edge of the stencil – this will stop the dye running out of the border.

Carefully remove the stencil and leave the mixture to dry – this can take up to two days, so be patient.

When the T-shirt is completely dry, mix up some cold-water dye according to the instructions on the pack.

Paint over your design using the brush. Be careful not to leave any gaps and not to go outside the border of your design. Leave the T-shirt to dry for another day.

When your design is completely dry, carefully peel off the paste and wash the T-shirt. At last, you can wear your unique T-shirt with pride.

Make A Cotton-Reel Snake

This toy snake slithers like a real snake, but the good news is that it won't ever bite.

You will need:

- 7 empty cotton reels
- a string of large beads
- a ping-pong ball • two corks
- a large darning needle and thick cotton
- a small piece of felt • glue • paints
- a hammer and nail

Thread the cotton on to the darning needle and tie a knot at one end. Feed the needle through one of the beads, then through a cotton reel.

Keep threading a bead and then a reel onto the string until all the reels have been used.

Make a hole in each of the corks by carefully hammering a nail into it lengthways then removing the nail. Now add a cork, a bead and another cork to the snake.

Use the needle to make two holes either side of the ping-pong ball. Run the needle through the ping-pong ball to make the snake's head. Then tie off the thread.

Cut out a tab of felt 2 cm long, and snip a V-shape out of one end. This is the snake's forked tongue. Glue the tongue to the head.

 Paint eyes and zigzag markings on the ball. Then decorate the reels in snaky colours.

Tie a length of string around the neck of the snake.

Once it has dried, grab hold of your snake and watch it slither.

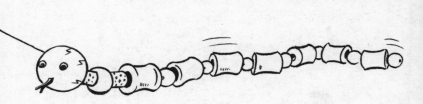

Deck The Halls With Homemade Garlands

Have a green Christmas with seasonal garlands made from rubbish and popcorn strings that the birds will enjoy when your festivities are over.

POPCORN STRINGS

Traditionally, strings of popcorn are used as decorations in the United States, where they have been hung on Christmas trees since the 19th century. As many an American bird knows, however, they also make excellent bird feeders when hung from a branch outside.

You will need:
- popping corn • a microwave or saucepan with lid
- a needle with a large eye
- strong thread or dental floss (unminted)

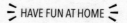 Pop lots of corn according to the packet instructions, especially if you want to eat some yourself, but remember to leave some for your feathered friends! Put aside to cool.

Cut your cotton or floss to double the length you want your popcorn string to be, and then thread it through the eye of the needle until the two ends are level. Tie a large knot at the end of the strands then, if your corn is cool enough, push the needle through the centre of the first piece.

Make sure the knot at the bottom is big enough to hold the popcorn on and then thread the popcorn on one at a time.

Continue until the string is almost full with a gap of 5 cm at the top. Then cut the thread to remove the needle and tie the loose ends into a knot.

Popcorn strings can go on your Christmas tree or decorate your mantelpiece. After Christmas use the thread at the top to tie the strings to a tree and give the birds a festive feast.

If you don't want to pop your own corn, you can use popcorn bought from the shop. However, avoid the salted variety – plain is best for the birds.

Top tip: Cranberries and blueberries also make an attractive and tasty addition to your popcorn strings.

GARLANDS OF PAPER BEADS

Transform rubbish into bright and colourful garlands that are very easy to make. The best bit is that you can find all the things you need around the house, so it even helps with the recycling.

You will need:

• strong thread or elastic • drinking straws
• old magazines • pen • ruler • threadable bits
and bobs – old buttons, beads, keys etc. • scissors
• paints and brushes • PVA or craft glue

To make the beads cut out lots of long triangles from a magazine. Make the base of each triangle as wide as you want the beads to be on your garland. Long triangles will make the beads thicker and shorter triangles will make them thin – a variety looks great.

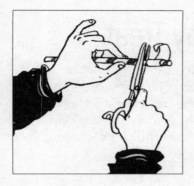

Next, cut lengths of straw the same length as the bases of your triangles. Then glue the base of each paper triangle to a straw section.

Wrap the rest of the triangle round the straw until you reach the tip. Glue the tip into place.

When the beads are dry, paint them in bright colours. Metallic paints can look great too, or they may look cool just as they are, in which case seal them with a coat of PVA glue.

Cut the thread or elastic to the length you want the garland, leaving a little extra for tying a knot. Thread on your beads, putting your buttons, keys, etc. at intervals along the string.

A Spa Day Treat

When a birthday or celebration comes around, or even if you just feel like it, what could be more special than creating your own personal health spa at home? There's no need to spend money on expensive skin-care products – you can make your own from the contents of the kitchen cupboard and fridge.

Whether it's for yourself, your parent, a friend or a sibling, put on your favourite relaxing music, wrap up in a cosy dressing gown and get ready for relaxation.

Warning: If you or anyone you're pampering has an allergy to any of the following ingredients, don't spread it on their skin. Make sure to check beforehand.

OATMEAL AND HONEY FACEPACK
You will need:

• 75 g (2¾ oz) oatmeal • 3 tbsp honey • 1 egg yolk

- -

Crack an egg over a bowl, keeping the yolk in one half of the shell. Pass the yolk from one half of the shell to the other, letting the white slip into the bowl below. When the shell contains just the yolk, tip this into another bowl and save the white to use for something else.

Add the rest of the ingredients to the egg yolk and stir until they are thoroughly mixed.

Use a clean paintbrush to apply the mixture to the face

of whoever you're pampering, using circular movements. Be careful to avoid the eye area. Leave it on for ten minutes. When the time is up, rinse off the facepack with warm water or cool rose water.

BANANA AND HONEY FACEPACK

Use a fork to mash a ripe banana. Add a teaspoonful of honey and mix together well.

STRAWBERRY FACEPACK

Mash four large strawberries and spread the pulp onto the skin.

COOLING CUCUMBER AND YOGURT FACEPACK

Purée a quarter of a cucumber in a blender and mix with a tablespoonful of plain yogurt – the sweetened fruit variety really doesn't work for this.

OLIVE OIL AND OATMEAL SCRUB
You will need:

- 2 tbsp ground uncooked oatmeal
- 1 tbsp olive oil • 1 tbsp lemon juice
- 1 tbsp brown sugar • 1 tsp of honey

Mix the ingredients together in a bowl and apply to the face with firm circular movements. Rinse off with warm water after ten minutes.

AVOCADO AND BANANA SCRUB
You will need:

- 1 dried avocado stone (left to dry for three days or more beforehand) • ½ ripe banana
- 1 tbsp olive oil • plastic bag and hammer

Place the avocado stone into a plastic bag (make sure it has no holes), then smash with a hammer until the pieces are fine. Mash the banana and mix it with the pit powder and olive oil. Apply with firm circular movements. Rinse off with warm water.

Top tip: After all of these treatments, splash cold water over the face to close the pores, and then pat dry with a clean towel.

Make Petal Perfume

All of the famous pop stars have a signature scent –
how about creating your own? Both girls and boys can
wear it or, if they're feeling generous, give it as a gift.
Hunting for the petals for your very own perfume is the
perfect way to pass the time if you're spending the day
around the house. Just be careful you're not tearing up
your parents' prize-winning dahlias.

CLASSIC ROSE PERFUME

Classic Rose Perfume will smell wonderful for a few days
but can go off quite quickly. Storing it in the fridge will
make it last longer and very refreshing to apply.

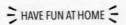

You will need:

- rose petals – as many as you can find
- 2 clean jars • an attractive glass bottle or scent bottle
- a strainer • water

Put the petals into the jar and add enough water to cover them and then about 1 cm more. Leave in a warm sunny spot for at least a day.

Wash the scent bottle with warm water and washing-up liquid, then rinse with a solution of water and a few drops of white vinegar. Be careful not to add too much, though, or your perfume could end up smelling very weird indeed.

Strain the petal water into a clean jar, squashing the petals to extract even more scent. Pour into the nice, clean bottle.

HEAVENLY BLOSSOM SCENT

This recipe will work well with any fragrant blossoms, but look out for lavender, honeysuckle and lilac as these are particularly good. This scent also has the advantage of keeping longer and will stay fresh for up to a month.

You will need:

- 2 cups of water • 1 cup of chopped petals or flowers
- 1 muslin or pudding cloth • a bowl
- white vinegar • a glass bottle

Lay the muslin in the bottom of the bowl so that the edges come over the side. Place the petals into the bowl and add water until the petals are completely submerged. Cover the bowl and leave overnight.

The following day, carefully lift the muslin out of the bowl, drawing the corners in to avoid dropping the petals. Gather up the corners and squeeze the water out of the muslin into a small clean saucepan, adding any water left in the bowl.

 Bring to the boil and simmer until a small amount of liquid (about a tablespoonful) is left, then remove from the heat and leave to cool.

Pour your scent into the bottle and add a pretty ribbon.

Create A Campfire Classic

You don't have to go far afield to enjoy a night under the stars. Why not set up camp right in your back garden? What is essential, however, is the classic campfire treat – s'mores.

To prepare s'mores, you'll need a campfire, but if you don't want a charred mess in the middle of your lawn, buy a disposable barbecue in a tray at your local supermarket or DIY store.

SUPER S'MORES

You will need:

- a packet of plain biscuits • a large bar of chocolate
- a bag of marshmallows • some metal skewers

Start by making sure your campfire or your barbecue is ready for cooking on. It is best when preparing s'mores to have a fire that is glowing rather than flaming.

Take two biscuits and add a couple of squares of chocolate to one of them.

Pop two marshmallows on to a skewer and hold them just above the flames of the campfire. Keep heating them until the marshmallows are golden brown and deliciously soft. The skewers might get very hot, so make sure you hold them at the end.

Warning: Make sure your marshmallows don't catch fire. If they do, quickly blow them out before they melt and fall off the skewer.

With the marshmallows still on the skewer, place them on top of the chocolate on the biscuit. Then take the other biscuit and make a sandwich. Squeeze the biscuits together as you pull out the skewer – leaving the marshmallows between the biscuits.

Wait until the marshmallows are cool enough to eat before you tuck in.

Delicious. Pass some more s'mores, please!

Make A Treasure Map

Why not make an ancient treasure map of your garden or local park? Bury some treasure where X marks the spot. Then see if the rest of the family can follow the map.

To make paper look like an ancient sheet of parchment, all you need to do is soak it in cold, strong black tea for about five minutes.

Remove the paper from the tea and spread it out onto a baking tray.

 Turn the oven onto the lowest heat. Place the baking tray in the bottom of the oven until the corners of the paper start to curl. Then carefully remove the tray from the oven using oven gloves.

Warning: When it is in the oven, a parent should keep a watchful eye on the map.

For a really authentic effect, use a quill to draw your map on the paper. Alternatively, draw your map in pen or pencil.

Add some islands and ships and draw a cross to mark where the treasure is hidden.

Shiver me timbers – a real treasure map!

Mind-Reading Together

This trick requires two people – one person is the mind-reader, the other is their assistant. The mind-reader must select a partner and impress the rest of the household with their incredible mind-reading abilities.

The assistant stands in front of the audience, and the mind-reader leaves the room. The assistant asks a member of the audience to choose an object in the room. They then tell the audience that the mind-reader will return to the room and be able to 'read' which item has been chosen.

HOW TO DO IT

In private, before the trick begins, the two performers must choose an item in the room to be their 'anchor' object. The mind-reader knows that the item that the audience selects will be the third thing that the assistant points to after pointing to the anchor.

For example, the performers choose a table as their anchor object. The mind-reader leaves the room and the audience chooses the TV as their object. The mind-reader returns and the trick goes as follows:

Assistant: *Is the object I am thinking of the rug on the floor here?*

Mind-reader: *No.*

Assistant: *Is it this table?* (Anchor)

Mind-reader: *No.*

Assistant: *Am I thinking of this chair?* (First)

Mind-reader: *No*

Assistant: *Am I concentrating on this vase?* (Second)

Mind-reader: *No*

Assistant: *Is the object I am thinking of this TV?* (Third)

Mind-reader: *Yes, it is.*

Great 'mind-readers' develop a slick and witty banter and put on a dramatic and somewhat over-the-top performance. But what they never, ever do, is reveal the secret of how their trick is done.

Play Giddy Running

The only thing more fun than getting as dizzy as you can and then trying to walk in a straight line is watching someone else do it. A good game for the garden, make sure you have lots of soft cushions so that you don't land with too much of a bump.

You will need:

- a large, flat grassy space in a garden or park
- lots of pillows and soft things to land on
- a broom handle or stick

- -

Lay the cushions out in two straight lines about a metre apart. This will mark the course.

Stand at the beginning of the course and hold the broom handle or stick to your chest vertically, so that the end of it comes about 30 cm above your head. Look up at the end of the broom and spin round as fast as you can five times. The other players should count out loud as you spin.

Stop when you are facing the beginning of the course and drop the broom carefully to the side. Now try to walk (or run) as fast as you can in a straight line to the end of the course. This is not as easy as you think, as you will now be very dizzy and will probably stumble as soon as you make a start.

The aim of giddy running is to get as far along the course as possible without touching the pillows at the side, and if you reach the end, to run back.

Classic Card Games

Playing cards is a great rainy-day activity that should never be forgotten or underestimated.

TWO-HAND WHIST

This simple form of whist can be played with two or more players. The dealer deals seven cards to each player and then cuts the pack to determine which suit is 'trumps'. The object of the game is to win as many 'tricks' as possible. A trick is where each player has had one turn. There are seven tricks available in each hand.

The other player (or the player to the left of the dealer if there are more than two of you) then lays a card in the middle of the table. Players must then lay a card of the same suit if possible and the highest card goes on to win the trick.

However, if a player can't follow suit they can lay any suit they like. If they lay a 'trump' i.e. any card from the trump suit, that card will beat all non-trump cards. A trump card can be beaten only by another, higher trump card. For example, if spades are trumps, a king of diamonds can be beaten by a two of spades. The two of spades can, in turn, be beaten by the three of spades or any higher spade.

The winner of the trick takes the cards and lays them face down on the table, and then leads the next trick.

Aces are always high. The winner of each round is the player who wins the most tricks.

KNOCKOUT WHIST

This game is exactly the same as Two-Hand Whist, except that you need more than two players, as any player who fails to win a trick is knocked out.

As a variation you can reduce the number of cards dealt by one each hand, starting at seven and reducing, eventually, to one.

The winner is the last surviving player when the others are knocked out.

UP AND DOWN THE RIVER

This game is based on whist but, instead of winning as many tricks as possible, you must predict the number of tricks you will win by looking at your hand.

For the first hand, the dealer deals one card each and then cuts to determine which suit is trumps. Each player must predict the number of tricks they can win (one or zero in this case) with the dealer bidding last. The total number of tricks predicted by each player MUST add up to either more or less than the possible amount for the hand. For example, if only one trick has already been bid for in round one, the dealer cannot bid zero, but must bid one no matter what their cards. This forces someone to lose the round.

If a player's prediction is right, he or she scores ten points plus the number of tricks bid. If their bid is over or under, the player scores only the amount of tricks won.

The number of cards dealt increases by one card each time, up to a total of seven.

After the round with seven cards is finished, there are several novelty rounds. Still playing with seven cards, try the following variations:

Half-blind. Players bid on their hand before they know the trump suit.

Blind. Players must bid before seeing their hand or cutting for trumps.

Misère. Three penalty points are deducted from a player's score for each trick they win, so you need to get as few as you can. Players who win no tricks gain ten points.

When these three rounds are finished, the game continues back 'down the river' from seven cards to one.

The winner is the player with the highest score.

Have A Plate-Spinning Competition

Plate spinning will keep you occupied for hours. Always use plastic plates – that way you won't break the best china and injure yourself in the process.

You will need:

- plastic plates with a circular rim underneath (they need a slightly hollow underside that slopes in towards the centre)
- bamboo sticks or dowelling (at least 1 m long)

- -

GOING SOLO

Start by holding a stick at a slight angle – imagine the angle an hour hand makes when it is pointing to two o'clock.

Pick up a plate and hang it from the stick by the rim.

Make a slow circular motion with your wrist, so that the plate starts to spin. Keep the rest of your arm still. Don't move your shoulder or elbow. Make sure the plate rolls around the stick, and doesn't get stuck on one spot. It should move like a spinning top, not a swinging lasso.

Gradually rotate the plate faster and faster until it levels out and is spinning horizontally. Then stop moving the stick. It should slide to the concave middle of the plate, and for the next few seconds, hey presto, the plate will spin by itself.

Don't panic when the plate starts to slow and wobble. Just give the stick a few more flicks with your wrist.

THE TWO TIMER

Now you've mastered the basic spin, switch the stick to your free hand by sliding your grip close to the plate, lifting your leg and handing the plate under your leg for extra effect. Then place another plate on the tip of a second stick, and spin the plates two-at-a-time. Watch that the plates don't collide with each other!

IN A SPIN

Kick off a contest to see who can spin a plate the longest. Then take your act outside and see who can spin the most plates at once. Push sticks into soft earth so you won't have to struggle to hold the plates as they spin.

As you set new plates spinning, give the other sticks a flick to keep them going.

If you manage to spin more than three plates at one time, congratulations – you should be in the circus!

TOP TRICKS

Lift the spinning plate off the stick with your forefinger and hold it up high. Then flick it up in the air and catch it on the end of your finger.

Spin two plates, one in each hand. Throw both plates into the air at the same time and then catch them on the opposite stick.

If you're feeling really clever, why not make the plate spin really quickly, tip your head back, and balance the end of the stick on your chin? Practice makes perfect.

Make Your Own Lemonade

On a baking hot summer's day there's nothing more refreshing than a large jug of homemade lemonade.

You will need:

- 7 lemons (to make a slightly sweeter drink, replace one of the lemons with a large orange)
- 350 g caster sugar • 1½ litres water
- runny honey to taste

- - - - - - - - - - - - - - - - - - - -

Grate the zest of two of the lemons into a large saucepan. Pour over 1½ litres of water and add the sugar.

 Heat the lemon, water and sugar mixture until all of the sugar has dissolved and leave to cool.

 Squeeze the juice of all the lemons into a large jug. Pour the cooled water over the lemon juice and stir.

Each time you make lemonade the flavour will be slightly different so always taste the mixture before serving. Stir in a teaspoon of honey if necessary. Add some ice cubes to the jug and serve.

Top tip: To make pink lemonade, add a cup of cranberry juice. This gives your drink a nice tang and makes it a lovely colour.

Bad Spelling Bee

Anyone can learn to spell well, but it takes talent to get words seriously wrong by spelling them as they sound. For example, if you tried hard enough, you could spell 'potato' 'ghoughpteighbteau'. Here's where the sounds for this awful spelling come from:

Letter	Sound	Example
P	gh	as in hiccou**gh**
O	ough	as in th**ough**
T	pt	as in **pt**erosaur
A	eigh	as in n**eigh**
T	bt	as in de**bt**
O	eau	as in bur**eau**

Or how about spelling 'usage' 'youzitch'. This packs seven errors into a five letter word. Can you beat that?

HOW TO PLAY

Ask an adult to challenge each player to come up with a word and devise the worst spelling they can for it. The players then have two minutes to come up with their final worst spelling and write it down.

The adult must then look at each player's word and guess what the word is even though it is badly spelt. Players score one point for each wrong letter they managed to fit into the word.

Good words to start with are: Australia, diamond, fatigue, height, leopard, mayonnaise, mnemonic, rhinoceros, xylophone and zucchini.

Hold A Gurning Championship

Believe it or not, there's a real art to looking ugly. In fact, there's even a world championship held every year to find the people who can pull the most horrible faces. This skill is called 'gurning', and it dates back hundreds of years.

Take a look in the mirror – have you got what it takes to be a world-champion gurner?

Find someone to act as an impartial judge. Then get gurning.

Disclaimer: The publisher takes no responsibility for the wind changing direction while you've got your gurning face on.

BASIC GURNING

There are three stages to pulling the basic gurning face:

1. Blow your cheeks out.

2. Suck air in through your nose.

3. Open your eyes wide and cross them.

Keep that face for several seconds, but don't freeze it. Make your muscles twitch, your eyes bulge, your neck veins stand out and your ears flap.

The judge then gives marks out of ten for each of these criteria:

- How long you can hold that ghastly look for.
- How much energy and animation shines through your gurning face.
- How completely your face is transformed by the gurn.

You get a 20 point bonus if you start off good-looking and gurn yourself into a gargoyle.

Did you know?
The World Gurning Championships are held at Egremont Crab Fair in the north-west of England. Competitors put their heads through a horse's harness and do their best gurning face. The fair has been held since 1267.

Some gurners take gurning so seriously that they have teeth removed to give their face more elasticity. They can achieve stomach-churning effects – like pulling both their lips over their nose – but this is not recommended.

Launch Orange Jelly Boats

Make dessert more exciting with a fantastic fleet of orange jelly boats. They're the perfect party dessert, you just have to add ice cream.

You will need:

- 3 oranges • 1 pack of fruit jelly
- 8 cocktail sticks • rice paper

- - - - - - - - - - - - - - - - - - -

Make the jelly with hot water, following the instructions on the pack. To make a firmer jelly only use ¾ of the water suggested on the pack. Leave to cool until it is lukewarm. You can speed this up by adding a few ice cubes.

Meanwhile, cut the oranges in half using a sharp knife, and begin to loosen their insides by cutting round the inside edges. Be very careful not to pierce the skin of the orange or you will not be able to pour jelly into them.

Scoop out the rest of the insides of the orange halves using a spoon, trying to remove as much of the white membrane as possible.

Keep the empty orange halves steady by placing them in a bun tin and then fill each one to the top with the warm jelly mix. Put the bun tin containing your orange jellies in the fridge to set.

While waiting for your jelly boats to set, make the sails. Cut triangles about 6 cm high out of the rice paper and thread with cocktail sticks to act as masts.

When the jelly has set, cut the oranges again so that they are now in quarters. Arrange them on a plate – a blue one is best, or cover a plate with foil to look like glistening waves.

You are now ready to put up your sails and drift into the sunset.

Put On A Magic Show

Stage a magic show for your family and friends and you'll have them gasping in awe at your magical powers. The great thing is that you can either be the magician, or the magician's assistant. Just make sure you practise the tricks thoroughly before you perform them in front of your audience. You don't want to be booed off stage!

MYSTICAL MAGIC EIGHTS

Here's a great card trick which will convince your audience you can read minds. You need any seven playing cards and the eight of clubs, a blindfold and the help of a volunteer from the audience who doesn't know how the trick works.

Decide which of you will be the magician and which will be the magician's assistant.

The magician deals out the eight cards face up on a table, so that they are arranged in the same pattern as the eight clubs on the eight of clubs card.

When the cards are laid out, the assistant then ties a blindfold over the magician's eyes.

The assistant asks for a volunteer from the audience and invites them to come up and select one of the eight cards and show it to the audience.

The volunteer then puts the card back in its place. All this is done in silence so that the magician cannot possibly guess which card was shown to the audience.

The magician removes the blindfold. The assistant points, seemingly at random, to the cards on the table. When the assistant points at the volunteer's chosen card, the magician shouts, '*I feel a strong vibe telling me that is your card*' – and it is!

WHAT'S THE SECRET?

To make this trick work, the assistant indicates to the magician which card was chosen in a very simple way. Before pointing to the chosen card, the assistant points a finger at the eight of clubs. He or she carefully touches one of the clubs on the face of the card. The one touched corresponds to the position of the chosen card in the layout of the eight cards. For example, if the ace was the chosen card, the magician would point to the club circled below on the eight of clubs.

A CRAFTY CARD TRICK

For the next trick, reverse roles so that the magician is now the assistant and the assistant is the magician.

The magician holds a pack of cards face down and shows the audience what they think is the card on the top of the pack.

Instead of lifting just the top card, the magician picks up the first and second card in one go – hiding the top card behind the second. (It is easier to lift the two cards in one go if, before the performance, you have bent them slightly. In private, practise lifting the cards smoothly and confidently.)

After the magician has shown the audience what is in fact the second card, he or she replaces both cards on top of the pack.

The magician holds out the deck of cards and the assistant takes the top card and slips it into the middle of the pack while telling the audience: 'I am placing the top card in the middle of the pack.'

The card that the audience was shown is now on the top of the pack.

The magician taps the pack and says 'Abracadabra!'

The magician's assistant then shows the audience the top card and they marvel in amazement, believing the card that they saw placed in the middle of the pack has magically returned to the top.

Play The Letter Chain Game

This is a great way to liven up a long day at home. It is suitable for players of all ages. You can have as many people competing as you like.

Start by picking a category (one that matches the ability of all the players). Younger players might suit a category such as animals or food. Slightly older players might jump at the chance to name films, celebrities or countries.

The youngest player starts the game by naming an example of something that fits into the category, such as 'dog', if the subject is animals.

The second youngest player must then name an animal which begins with the last letter of the previous answer. For example: 'giraffe', because 'g' is the last letter of dog.

This continues until all players have given an answer in ascending order of age.

If a player gets stumped by his or her letter, they are out. The winner is the last person left in the game.

Play can then start again with a whole new subject and a whole new letter chain. Let your imagination run riot!

Top tip: When you've worked your way through all the obvious categories, experiment with a wide range of weird and wonderful subjects. How about imaginary creatures or storybook characters?

Have A Thumb-Wrestling Contest

Thumb wrestling might be one of the world's smallest sports, but it requires bags of energy and concentration. In this frantic game, lock hands with an opponent and try to pin down their thumb, without your own thumb getting trapped. The winner is the person who pins down their opponent's thumb the greatest number of times in one game.

RULE OF THUMB

• Before the match starts, agree the number of rounds that will be played. Each round ends when a thumb is pinned down by another thumb for at least four seconds.

• Decide whether forefingers are allowed to wrestle as well as thumbs. It is easier if your forefinger 'snakes' around your opponent's top knuckle to help hold their wriggly thumb, so if you want to keep fingers out of the match, agree on the following pledge:

'No snakes, no buddies and no tag teams.'

This means neither contestant is allowed to move any fingers, just their thumb.

• Remember, this isn't an arm wrestling competition. Your elbows and wrists must not move.

IN THE RING

To make a professional-looking thumb-wrestling ring you will need a piece of sturdy cardboard or light wood.

 Cut two holes for the thumbs about 4 cm apart. If using wood, smooth the edges of the holes with sandpaper to avoid painful splinters.

LET THE GAME BEGIN

Make sure both players understand and agree the rules in advance, so there is less chance of an argument developing.

Sit down at a table, with your chair facing your opponent.

Both players must wrestle using the same hand – right hand to right hand, or left hand to left hand.

Bend the chosen hand to make a curved C-shape without any gaps between your fingers. Keeping your hand in this position, link 'Cs' with your opponent, with the underside of your fingers touching.

Press the tips of your thumbs together and start the game by chanting a rhyme such as:

'One, two, three, four, I declare a thumb war!
Five, six, seven, eight, try to keep your thumb straight.'

Throughout the chant, each contestant repeatedly moves their thumb either side of their opponent's thumb. As soon as the chant has ended, the match begins. Wriggle, twiddle, bend and twist your thumb to snare the other player's thumb and pin it down for a count of four, chanting *'One, two, three, four, I won the thumb war!'*

Repeat until an agreed number of rounds have been played, or until someone is scared they might dislocate their thumb!

If all else fails, do your best to distract your opponent by making them laugh or lose their concentration. It's totally above board and part of the fun of thumb wrestling.

Top tip: Why not give each thumb a bandanna by tying a tiny strip of different coloured material around its top.

Awesome Stained-Glass Window Biscuits

Here's how to create a stunning piece of edible art inside a biscuit. Unleash your imagination as you design your dazzling 'windows'.

You will need:

- 100 g (4 oz) caster sugar • 100 g (4 oz) butter or margarine • 225 g (9 oz) plain flour
- ½ tsp vanilla extract • juice and rind of ½ a lemon
- 1 egg yolk • boiled sweets in a selection of colours

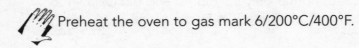 Preheat the oven to gas mark 6/200°C/400°F.

Grease two baking sheets. Put the butter or margarine and the sugar into a large bowl, and mix together with a wooden spoon. When the mixture is soft and a light-yellow colour, add the flour, vanilla extract, grated lemon rind and the juice – then stir all the ingredients together.

Beat the egg yolk in a small bowl and then add it to the mixture. Combine to make a nice dough. Cover the dough in plastic wrap and put it in the fridge for about 25 minutes.

Remove the dough from the fridge and on a very lightly floured surface, roll it out until it is about 1 cm thick.

Cut out your biscuits using a variety of cutter shapes.

Make a hole in each biscuit for a 'stained-glass window'. Experiment by cutting out various window shapes – try squares, hearts, circles, and even triangles. Use mini-cutter shapes if you have them. Place the biscuits on the baking sheets.

Pop the biscuits in the oven and bake for six minutes. Then remove from the oven.

Now for the fun bit. Place a sweet in each of the cut-out shapes (being careful not to burn your hands on the hot biscuits or baking sheets).

Put the biscuits back in the oven and cook for four more minutes or until the sweets start to melt. Remove the biscuits from the oven. Place on a wire rack and leave to cool.

Take a step back and admire your stained-glass treats.

Top tip: Stained-glass window biscuits make beautiful Christmas tree decorations. Make a hole in the top of each one before baking. When the biscuits have cooled, thread ribbon through the holes and tie them to your tree.

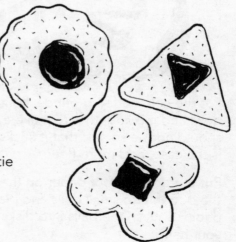

Create Your Own Fantastic Fossils

Create your very own dinosaur and footprint fossils.

You will need:

- a plastic dinosaur (shells, twigs and leaves make great fossils too)
- a small cup full of cold coffee grounds
- 175 ml cold water • 210 g flour • 6 tbsps salt
- a baking tray • greaseproof paper

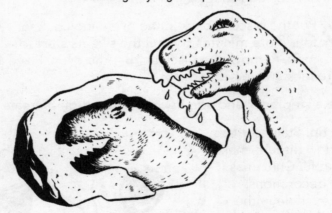

Put the cold coffee grounds, flour, salt and water in a bowl and mix together to make a dough. The dough should not be so soft that it sticks to your fingers. If this is the case, add more flour.

Put the greaseproof paper on the baking tray. Break the dough into small balls and place them on top of the paper. Squash the balls into disks with the palm of your hand.

Turn your toy dinosaur sideways and press it into each disk of dough. Then carefully peel it out to leave perfect dino-imprints.

 Bake the fossils at a low heat until they are hard. When they come out they will look delicious, but don't be tempted to eat them!

FOOTPRINT FOSSILS

You will need:

• modelling clay • a hard-boiled egg (in its shell) • a pencil • plaster of Paris • greaseproof paper

- - - - - - - - - - - - - - - - - - -

Knead the clay and roll it out into a thick, flat disc. Make a raised rim around the edge of the disc by pressing a long sausage-shaped piece of clay around the rim.

Press the bottom of an egg into the clay – then lift it out. The imprint made is the middle of the dinosaur's foot. With your finger make four toe imprints around the foot.

Use a pencil to scratch out a vicious claw at each toe-tip.

Mix a cup of plaster of Paris in a bowl with half a cup of water, and stir it into a soupy paste. Pour the paste into the hollow footprint, making sure there are no air bubbles. Leave to set, then peel the clay away from your footprint.

Get 'Tuned In'

'Tuned In' is a game that costs absolutely nothing to play. All you need is a radio, a timer or stopwatch, and some paper and pens.

HOW TO PLAY

Each player takes it in turns to tune the radio to a random channel and leaves it there for 10 seconds. That player scores points depending on what is being broadcast on the channel they have selected. The winner is the person who scores the most points in one hour.

Top tip: You might also like to keep a blindfold handy to stop players peeking at the frequency of the radio as they turn the dial or change the channel.

This table shows the points awarded for each subject the radio might be playing. If there is an overlap of subjects during those 10 seconds, it is the first subject that counts.

• **Music:** 1 point
Bonus: An extra 3 points if you can name the song or piece of music and 5 more if you can sing or hum the next line

• **News:** 2 points
Bonus: 5 extra points if the player can explain what the news story is about

• **Foreign Language:** 3 points
Bonus: An extra 3 points if you can name the language

• **Adverts:** 3 points
Bonus: 5 points if you've ever bought the product

• **Classical Music:** 4 points

• **A Jingle:** 5 points
Bonus: 10 points for singing the whole jingle yourself

• **A Weather Report:** 5 points

• **Sports Match:** 5 points

• **Phone-in:** 5 points
Bonus: 10 extra points if you can give an instant opinion on the topic

• **Traffic Report:** 5 points

Once you've learned how to play the basic version of 'Tuned In', try these variations:

Radio Bingo: Each player has their own piece of paper with a list of all of the categories shown opposite. When a player tunes into one of the categories they can cross it off their list.

The winner is the first person to cross off each of the categories. They can then shout: *'I'm tuned in!'*

In A Spin: Before play begins, draw a large circle on a piece of A4 paper, and divide it into ten segments.

Write the name of one category in each of the sections.

Then using a pen as a spinner, one player spins to select the 'instant loser' category.

Now, wearing a blindfold, take it in turns to choose a channel. If a player chooses a station that is broadcasting the instant loser programme they are automatically out of the game.

Continue until only one person remains.

Play Gods And Goddesses

This is a great game to get your mental cogs turning and to test you and your family's general knowledge.

Each player needs a sheet of paper and a pen. Divide the paper into a grid, with 11 rows and two columns. At the top of the left-hand column write 'Category' and at the top of the right-hand column write 'Word'.

Now each player picks a category in turn and all players write them into the boxes in the left-hand column. Typical categories include TV programmes, authors, pop stars, trees, flowers or, even the Gods and Goddesses of ancient history.

When ten categories are filled in, a letter is picked at random by someone sticking a pencil into the page of a newspaper, magazine or book with their eyes closed. Whichever letter the pencil is either touching or nearest to is the chosen letter for the round.

Timing with a watch or timer, one player says 'Go'. Players now have two minutes to fill in as many of the categories as they can with answers beginning with the chosen letter.

Where the answer is a person's name, the surname should begin with the correct letter.

On the next page there is an example of what the sheet may look like.

The chosen letter is 'S'.

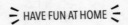

CATEGORY	WORD
Trees	Sycamore
Popstars/groups	Taylor Swift
Film stars	Emma Stone
Authors	William Shakespeare
Books	Swallows and Amazons
Gods and Goddesses	Saturn
Countries	Spain
Animals	Sheep
TV programmes	Sesame Street
Flowers	Snowdrop

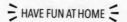

If anyone fills their sheet in before the 2 minutes are up, they can shout 'Stop' and the round ends. Otherwise all players must stop writing after 2 minutes.

Scores are determined by the number of people who have the same answer as you for each category. The top score is ten but one point is knocked off for each person who duplicates your answer. E.g. if three people have the answer 'Snowdrop', each player only scores seven for that answer.

A new letter is then chosen for the next round.

Make A Button Yo-Yo

You can create a nifty, personalized yo-yo with just two large coat buttons (look for two that are at least 2 cm wide) and some extra-strong thread.

Cut 50 cm of thread and, holding the buttons back to back, lace the thread back and forth between all of the holes. Keep going until the buttons are securely tied together with a slight gap between them.

Push the thread through one of the holes and pull it out between the two buttons. Loop it three times around the cotton core, then knot it securely on itself.

Tie a loop in the other end of the thread that is large enough for you slip your middle finger through. If you are right-handed, use the middle finger of your right hand, and the opposite if you're left-handed.

Wind the thread of your yo-yo around the core until it is wound all the way up to the loop and you can hold the yo-yo in your palm.

LET'S GO AND YO-YO

Flip your fingers down and let the yo-yo roll off them. As it falls, turn your hand over, jerk the thread and snatch the yo-yo as it comes back up.

Make A Denim Kit Bag

Denim bags are great, lightweight, washable holdalls, useful for whatever you need to carry. You don't even have to buy one in the shops, instead you can create one out of an old pair of jeans. Just make sure that you're not accidentally recycling someone's prized pair of designer denims!

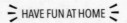

You will need:

- an old pair of jeans • scissors • chalk or pen
- ruler • brightly coloured cotton or silk scarf
- optional embellishments

Zip up the jeans and turn them inside out. Lay them out flat in front of you, bottom side up, and measure 2½ cm down the leg from the crotch.

With chalk, draw a line across the leg at this mark and repeat for the other leg. Cut the legs off at the line you have drawn.

Sew each leg closed 2½ cm from the cut edge. Trim the seam to 1 cm, then turn the bag so it is right side out.

To make a handle, thread a brightly coloured scarf through the belt loops and tie the ends together. Alternatively, cut the two inside seams from the leftover legs of the jeans and sew onto both sides of the bag to make long handles.Now add any embellishments you like, such as fabric football badges, swimming or gymnastic awards as well as buttons or ribbons. Stitch them into place for a truly original design.

Make A Rainstick

A rainstick is a South American musical instrument made from a cactus filled with hundreds of fragments, such as seeds and small stones. When the stick is turned upside down the seeds make a sound like raindrops falling on leaves. Native South Americans believe this sound encourages the gods to make it rain. Here's how to make a rainstick without a cactus.

You will need:

• cardboard tubes, the sturdier the better
• carpet tacks with flat heads • seeds, beads, lentils, or even pieces of gravel • cardboard • shells and straws to decorate your rainstick • paints • sticky tape

Tape your tubes together to make a long, hollow 'stick'.

 Push or hammer carpet tacks into your stick in a spiral pattern stretching from one end of the tube to the other. The more tacks you use, the noisier your rainstick will be, but make sure that the points of the tacks don't stick through the other side of the stick.

Cut a circle of cardboard and tape it over one end of the stick to seal it. Now pour in handfuls of seeds, lentils, gravel and beads. Seal the other end with another circle of cardboard so that the contents will not fall out all over the floor, making you unpopular with your parents.

Paint your rainstick with bright tropical colours. Why not add shell patterns and some feathers cut from coloured paper?

For the best effect, don't shake the rainstick. Simply turn it on one end and let the contents trickle through the spikes. Then turn it over again, like an egg timer. Wait and see if it rains!

Brilliant Butterfly Magnets

Use coffee filters to make the multicoloured wings of a butterfly. The resulting butterflies can be made into a fridge magnet or a brooch, or clipped onto curtains or fabric around the house.

You will need:

• a round coffee filter • food colouring in
various colours • a pipette or small paintbrush • cake tin
• clean yogurt pots or any small containers •
• pipe cleaners • a wooden clothes peg •
• black or brown paint • small magnet or magnetic
strip, or safety pin (for brooch) • strong glue

- - - - - - - - - - - - - - - - - - -

In the yogurt pots or small containers, mix six drops of food colouring with a few drops of water (make sure you don't dilute it too much).

Put a coffee filter in the bottom of a cake tin. Using the pipette or paintbrush, drip the coloured water onto the filter, allowing it to spread.

Do the same with another colour, then another and so on, making different coloured blobs all over the paper. Leave to dry.

Paint the clothes peg black or brown and leave to dry.

Fold a pipe cleaner into a V-shape and glue to the flat end of the clothes peg (the bit you pinch). This forms the antennae of the butterfly.

Scrunch the filter in the middle, to form wings and then clip the clothes peg onto the middle. Tease the paper into wing shapes.

Glue magnetic tape or a magnet to the back of your butterfly and stick it on the fridge. Alternatively, attach a safety pin using sticky tape to make a brooch.

If you can't find any safety pins (because no one can find a safety pin when they need one), clip the clothes peg to your curtains.

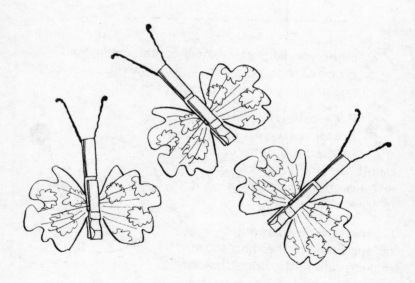

Build A Teepee

Instead of putting that boring old tent up in the garden again, impress your friends and neighbours by building a Sioux teepee. Take turns to be chief!

You will need:

- a dozen bamboo canes about 2 m long
- strong twine • old sheets or blankets • a stepladder
- safety pins • clothes pegs

Take three canes and lay them on the ground. Knot twine around the top of the canes to tie them into the shape of a tripod.

Lift up the tripod and push the canes apart so that they balance. Lean the other canes around the tripod, spacing them evenly.

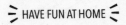 Using a stepladder to reach, tie all your canes together at the top with twine. Now arrange the canes to form a circular base approximately 2½ m in diameter. Widen the gap between two canes to act as a doorway.

Grab your blankets or sheets and start pegging them to the canes. Start at the bottom of the teepee, and work your way to the top. Don't forget to leave a gap for the entrance.

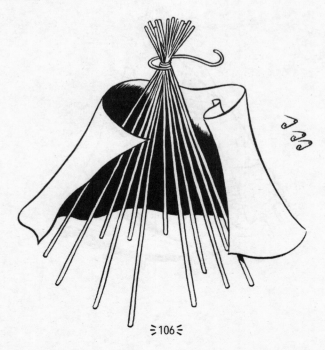

Use safety pins to hang a strip of the cloth across your entrance.

Now you are ready to have a powwow in your teepee. Why not make up a sign language to communicate with each other?

Friends

Hold out one arm with the hand open.

Winter

Cross both arms and shiver.

Our Family

Thump your chest above your heart with a clenched fist.

Make Bird-Cake Bells

Attract feathered friends to your garden with these easy-peasy bird-cake bells. Hang them in a tree and watch as birds flock to these fatty feasts.

You will need:

• birdseed • peanuts • grated cheese • 500 g lard
• string (around 30 cm long) • two yogurt pots (washed)

Before you start, soften the lard by standing it at room temperature for an hour or so.

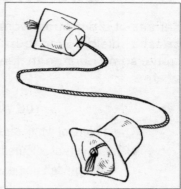

Make a small hole in the bottom of each of your yogurt pots with a skewer or scissors. Thread your string through the two holes and pull far enough to tie a knot on the inside length. Make the knots big enough so as not to slide through the holes.

Cut the lard into small pieces and put it in the mixing bowl. Add half of the seeds, nuts and cheese and knead them into the fat with your fingers. When the mixture is combined add the rest of the ingredients and keep kneading until the lard holds the mixture together.

Squash the mixture into the yogurt pots and place in the fridge to set.

After an hour or so check that the fat has set. Then carefully cut away the yogurt pots. Hang the bird-cake bells over the branch of a tree or from a bird table.

From a discreet distance keep an eye out for feathered visitors and keep a good bird book handy so you can identify your dinner guests as they arrive.

Top tip: Always hang bird-cake bells. Don't let them sit on a bird table or windowsill – this might attract unwanted cats and rats.

Become A Knight

Knights of old proudly wore their family's coat of arms on their shield during jousting matches. Here's how to create some bunting that includes your own family's coat of arms.

You will need:

- a piece of white card at least 40 cm by 50 cm
- large sheets of coloured paper in at least two colours
- string • felt-tip pens • masking tape • glue
- a ruler • scissors

- - - - - - - - - - - - - - - -

Draw a shield shape on to the white card, 35 cm wide and 45 cm long. Use a ruler to draw two lines 5 cm apart across the middle of the shield. Start the first line about 20 cm down from the top.

Now use a pair of scissors to cut out your shield.

SYMBOLS OF THE KNIGHT

Dream up two designs that symbolize your family. For example, if your surname is Smith, you could draw a horseshoe in the top half of the shield. If it is Mann, you could draw a man. If there's an artist in the family, you could try drawing a palette with a brush, or you could use one of your parent's jobs or the household pet for inspiration.

For the bottom half of the shield, choose a design inspired by an activity you enjoy together. For example, draw waves if you love visiting the beach, a tennis racket or football if you are sports fans, or a castle if you love visiting historic places.

To finish off your coat of arms, shade the three sections of the shield in different colours. How about red in the top section, green at the bottom and yellow in the stripe?

Measure a length of string that will span the room you want to hang the bunting across. Cut it just long enough so that it hangs down in a gentle arc. Pierce a hole in the top two corners of your shield and thread the shield onto the string, pulling it into the middle.

TIME TO ADD SOME BUNTING

No knight's debut would be complete without lots and lots of multi-coloured bunting.

Take some sheets of coloured paper that match the colours on your shield and cut them into strips, 30 cm by 15 cm.

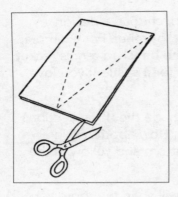

Fold the strips in half lengthways and cut a V-shape from the open base to form a pennant. Repeat with different colours of paper.

Open out the folded shapes and put a thin line of glue on the inside of the folds before gluing the pennants on to your string.

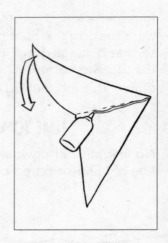

Add more pennants side-by-side along your bunting until the string is full. Then hang it across the room, securing the ends with masking tape.

Congratulations. You have been knighted!

Rustle Up A Leafy Scene

The vibrant reds and yellows of leaves when they start to fall from the trees make woods and gardens look beautiful, and can also make a stunning work of art.

Choose a crisp, blue-skied day and go out into the garden or for a walk in the park. Leaves can be found just about anywhere there are trees and nobody minds if you pick them up off the ground. Make sure you dust off any bugs before you put them in your bag.

Collect as many different shapes and colours as you can.

PRESERVING LEAVES

You will need:

- a variety of leaves • wax paper
- acrylic craft spray from a craft shop • an iron

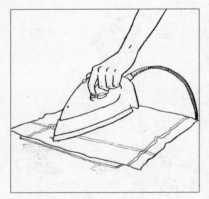

Place the leaves between two layers of wax paper and cover with an old towel or piece of cloth.

Iron the fabric with the iron on a warm setting. This will seal the sheets of wax paper together with the leaf in between.

Cut around the shape of your leaf, leaving a narrow margin of wax paper around the leaf edge.

Set aside your leaves for a day or two and then spray them with a sealant, such as acrylic craft spray.

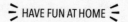

PRESSING LEAVES

If you can't find any wax paper, don't despair. You can still make a marvellous picture by pressing the leaves between the pages of a large book.

You will need:

• a variety of leaves • some sheets of newspaper
• a large heavy book • some other books to rest on top

Place each leaf between two sheets of newspaper and press between the pages of the large book.

Leave at least a ½ cm of book pages between each leaf you press. When the book is full of leaves, shut it and place more books on top for extra pressure.

Leave these for about two weeks and then remove each leaf carefully.

THE PICTURE

When the leaves are ready, you can create a picture. Take a sheet of paper and experiment with where to position the leaves. Some leaves make great fish shapes. When you are happy with your design, stick the leaves down with PVA glue and leave to dry.

Make A Prickly Hedgehog

This pin-covered pet is a practical pal in anyone's sewing box. Either keep him all to yourself, or give him to a friend or relative. He may look cute but don't give him a cuddle or you could get pricked.

You will need:

- black and brown felt
- 2 buttons or teddy bear eyes from a craft shop
- scissors • chalk • needle and black thread
- tracing paper and pencil
- old tights or more fabric scraps for stuffing

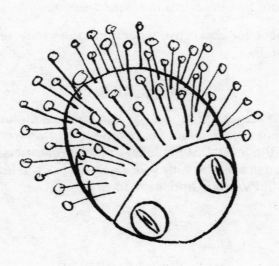

First you need to make the pattern for your prickly friend. Place the tracing paper over the pattern below and draw around it using a pencil. Trace around each shape separately so that you end up with three shapes on your paper. Cut these out carefully using scissors.

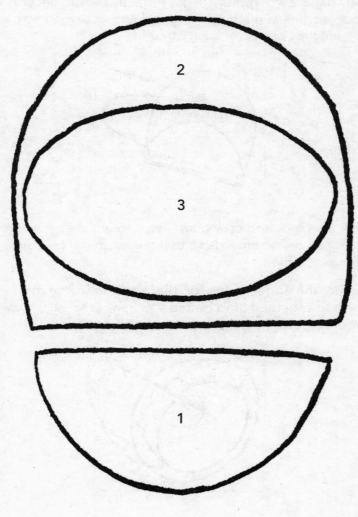

Place shape 1 onto a piece of black felt and draw around it with chalk. Repeat this on the brown felt with shapes 2 and 3 and then cut out your shapes.

Using running stitch (see page 37), sew felt shape 1 to felt shape 2 along the straight edge as shown. Secure your stitches at the beginning and end of sewing with a few stitches on top of each other.

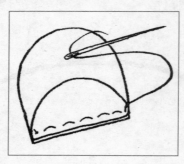

Sew the black and brown top piece to felt shape 3 with the seam facing inwards so that the seam will be inside your pincushion.

Gather the edges of the top piece as you sew to make them fit together. Stop before you have sewn all the way around, leaving hole to insert the stuffing.

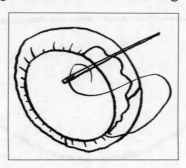

Fill your cushion with stuffing until it is firm and then sew up the hole.

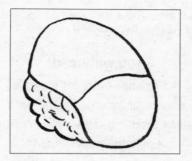

Sew on the buttons for your hedgehog's eyes.

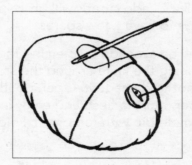

All that's missing now are his prickles, so fill the hedgehog with all of your pins.

Grow An Avocado Plant

Avocados make beautiful indoor plants and will grow from the stone of the fruit you eat.

You will need:

- a few ripe avocados • a knife
- some jars or wide-necked bottle
- water • cocktail sticks • a 15 cm plant pot
- potting compost • sand

- - - - - - - - - - - - - - - - -

Top tip: Not all avocado stones will grow into successful plants so it pays to have a few spares.

Cut open an avocado by piercing the skin and then running the knife around the stone, being careful not to damage it. Open gently and remove the stone. Scoop out the flesh and enjoy later – perhaps make a guacamole dip with red onion, lime juice, chilli and coriander.

Wash the stone and insert three cocktails sticks into its side. The cocktail sticks should be evenly spaced and about halfway down from the widest end.

Using the cocktail sticks as a rest, suspend the stone pointed side up, in a jar filled with water. Place the jar on a warm windowsill. Keep the jar filled to the brim with water at all times, so that half of the stone is underwater.

In two or three weeks, the stone will crack. In another four weeks a root will grow from the submerged end. Shortly afterwards a stem will begin to grow.

When the root is at least 5 cm long and the stem is at least 10 cm tall, plant the stone in a pot measuring 15 cm or more in diameter. Good potting soil should be used – mix three parts of soil with one part of sand. The pot should be kept wet for the first week. After that the soil should be watered once a week and kept moist.

Avocado plants can grow into small bushes or taller trees. Which one is up to you. If you want a bush, pinch off the tip of the plant. If you would prefer a small tree, just let it grow upwards.

Don't wait around for your plant to bear fruit though, as it could take years or it may never happen at all.

Grow Your Name In Cress

Every year, parks and stately homes spend huge amounts of money on elaborate floral displays. Primroses and pansies are planted in the shape of mermaids, whales and ships. Some towns use flowers to spell out their names across flowerbeds. It's time to achieve the same effect for your family – albeit on a smaller scale – by writing your names in cress.

You will need:

- a packet of cress seeds • an old hand towel
- a sheet of paper • plastic wrap • a baking tray

Wet the towel with warm water, so that it's damp but not soaking wet. Lay it flat on the tray.

Fold your sheet of paper in half and sprinkle seeds along the fold so it is easy to pour the seeds accurately.

Tipping the paper carefully, pour a stream of seeds on to the towel, spelling out your name. If your name is super-long you could just do your initials or nickname, otherwise you will need to find a beach towel!

Cover the tray with a length of plastic wrap and seal it around the edges.

Place the tray somewhere warm where it can get a little sunlight, and leave it there for two days. After that time, take the plastic wrap off the towel and water it slightly.

Leave the towel uncovered and place it in a really sunny spot (but not glaring sunlight). The cress will begin to grow – don't forget to water it now and again.

Make the most of your crop by harvesting it and serving it in a sandwich with a sliced hard-boiled egg!

Make A Dream Catcher Mobile

Native Americans believed that dreams travelled through the air before reaching sleepers. They hung dream catchers up to stop bad dreams from coming their way. The nightmares got caught in the webs, while the good dreams slid off the feathers at the bottom and dropped softly on to the sleepers below.

You will need:

- a netting fruit bag • coloured wool
- a round plastic lid from an ice cream container
- beads • coloured feathers (available at craft shops and some supermarkets) • scissors
- craft glue • a hairgrip

- -

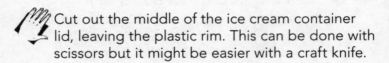 Cut out the middle of the ice cream container lid, leaving the plastic rim. This can be done with scissors but it might be easier with a craft knife.

Pull the netting tightly over the rim, then tie together at the back.

Using the hairgrip as a needle, wind the wool tightly round the outside of the hoop and through the mesh until the rim is covered. Then tie the ends of the wool together. Tie a loop of wool to the top of the hoop to hang it up.

Cut away the rough ends of the netting at the back of your dream catcher using scissors.

Cut three strands of wool, about 60 cm long, for the beads. Double the strands over and tie the folded ends to the sides and middle of the dream catcher. Make sure the loose ends hang down. Then add your beads. Tie a large knot in the wool to keep the beads on.

Now glue a feather to the bottom of each strand.

The dream catcher needs to be suspended within a few feet of the bed and able to move freely. If possible, it is best to hang it from the ceiling. Sweet dreams!

Make A Gorgeous Gift

This beautiful bath buff-puff is the perfect gift for you or someone in your family, because not only does it look lovely, it's very useful at bathtime for lathering up soap and shower gel.

Choose a pretty colour of netting and a matching ribbon to create a great gift.

You will need:

- 1 m soft tulle or netting • a needle with a large eye
- thread in a matching colour to the tulle
- ½ m pretty ribbon • pins

Spread the netting out flat. Fold the fabric over 12 cm up from the bottom edge. Fold over again and again until all the tulle has been folded into a tube 12 cm wide.

Secure the fabric with pins, and then sew along the centre of the tube from one end to the other using running stitch (see page 37).

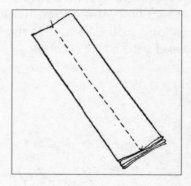

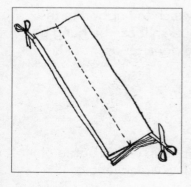

Once you have sewn along the length of the tulle, cut along both edges.

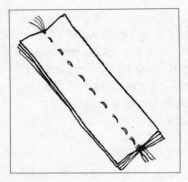

Using a loose running stitch, sew along the length of the tulle again, without securing your stitches at the end. The thread needs to be very strong for this so try quadrupling your thread (so that you are sewing with four strands instead of one).

Pull on the thread so that the tulle gathers together in a long ruffle. Secure at the end with a few stitches.

Finally stitch the two ends together to form a loop.

Attach the ribbon to the puff so it can be hung out to dry after use.

Now all you need to do is wrap it up with a bottle of bubbles and present it to the lucky recipient.

Create Your Own Solar System

Here's your chance to create a whole solar system of your own – one that's tiny enough to fit in your house!

You will need:

- 5 tennis balls • 5 ping-pong balls • poster paints and brushes
- duct tape • eye hooks • a sheet of white card
- three 1 metre-long wooden sticks • a ball of wool
- a long darning needle • a craft knife

- - - - - - - - - - - - - - - - - - - -

Get to work with your paints to transform the tennis balls into planets. Paint them different colours – one could have swirls of red to show electrical storms battering the planet. One could have clouds and continents. You can model your planets on the real planets in our own solar system, or you can make up your own – it's your choice.

Why not cut out a ring of card and push it over one of the balls to represent rings (like those that circle Saturn in our own solar system)? Secure the card with duct tape and spatter the ball and the ring with paint dots.

Paint one tennis ball bright orange, because this will be the star at the centre of your solar system.

Now make some smaller planets from the ping-pong balls. Again, paint them exactly as you like, making each one different.

GET MOBILE

To make the frame of your mobile, cut one of the metre-long sticks in half.

Then use some wool to bind the two 50 cm lengths together, into the shape of a cross.

Make another cross using the other metre-long stick.

Then bind the two crosses together into an eight-pointed star (as shown in the picture opposite). This is the frame on which your solar system will be suspended.

Next, you need to attach the planets to the frame. Thread a length of wool through a long darning needle and tie a big knot in the end. Push the needle through a ping-pong ball and tie it to one of the sticks. Repeat for the other four ping-pong balls.

To add the tennis balls to your frame, screw an eye hook into each one of the balls. Attach a length of wool to each eye hook and suspend the tennis balls from the sticks of your frame.

Hang the fifth orange tennis ball that represents your star from the middle of the mobile's frame, where the sticks cross. This star forms the centre of your solar system, just like the Sun that sits at the centre of our own solar system.

Hang your mobile from the ceiling and push the planets around until the whole structure balances. Then stand back and admire your creation.

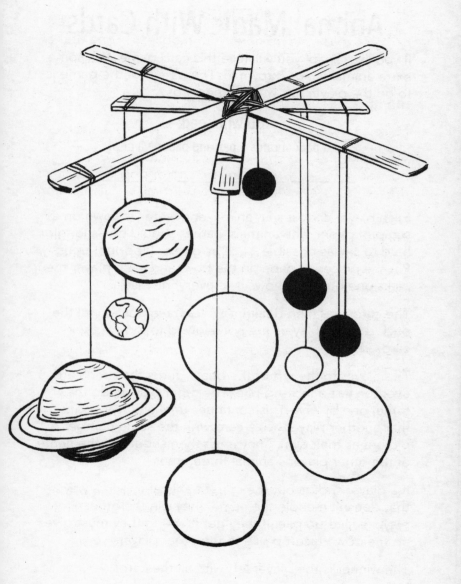

Animal Magic With Cards

If you like 'Snap' you will love this card game with some extra animal chaos thrown in. The object of the game is to be the player left with all the cards.

You will need:

• a pack of cards • pen and paper • a bowl

- - - - - - - - - - - - - - - - - -

Each player chooses an animal and writes it down on a scrap of paper. The animals' names should be as long or hard to say as possible, such as gnu or hippopotamus. Put the pieces of paper in the bowl and each player then picks one out and shows it to everyone else.

The cards are then dealt into piles, face down until the pack is gone. Players are not allowed to look at their cards just yet.

The player to the left of the dealer turns their top card over to start a face-up pile. The other players do the same, one by one. This continues until a player spots that another player has a card with the same number or picture as their own. They must then shout out the name of the other player's animal three times.

If a player shouts out the correct animal and in a way that doesn't mangle the name, they win the other player's face-up pile. If they get it wrong they must give up their own face-up pile to the other player.

The winner is the player left with all the cards.

Create A Magic Wheel

Back in Victorian times, there weren't any films or computer games. A 'zoetrope', or 'magic wheel', was the nearest thing to TV. Here's how to make one of your own.

You will need:

- a piece of cardboard (25 cm by 25 cm)
- a large sheet of coloured paper (at least 70 cm by 22 cm)
- a strip of white paper (70 cm by 6 cm)
- felt-tip pens • two 30 cm-long dowelling rods
- a ruler • sticky tape • glue • a pair of scissors
- a pair of compasses • a piece of string 2 m long

--- --- --- --- --- --- --- ---

Use a pair of compasses to draw a circle on the cardboard 21 cm in diameter. Cut the circle out.

Take the coloured paper and cut three strips 70 cm in length. Make one strip 5 cm wide, one 7 cm wide and one 10 cm wide.

Take the 10 cm-wide strip and cut it into 15 sections – each 4 cm wide. Firmly glue the short edges of the strips along the length of the 7 cm-wide strip, leaving a gap of a ½ cm between each strip. You should have a short gap at the end.

Now take the 5 cm-wide strip, and glue it securely along the top of the sections. This will be your viewing wheel.

With the 7 cm strip at the bottom, cut 1 cm notches along the lower edge. Curve your viewing wheel around the cardboard circle, folding the notches over. Use tape and glue to fix 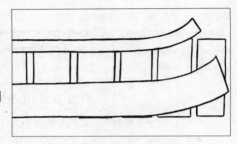 the circle in place. You will also need to tape the top strip to complete the cylinder.

Take the strip of white paper that is 70 cm by 6 cm. This will make your movie sequence strip.

Draw 15 figures, evenly spaced along the strip. Make each picture slightly different — if you were showing a man running, his arms and legs would be in a slightly different position in each picture. Slide this picture strip inside the slatted frame and push it back against the frame so it runs all the way round, like wallpaper.

Pierce two holes, opposite each other, in the top of the paper frame and slide one of the dowelling rods through both holes. Do the same with the other rod, fractionally lower and at right angles to the first. The two rods will form a cross in the middle.

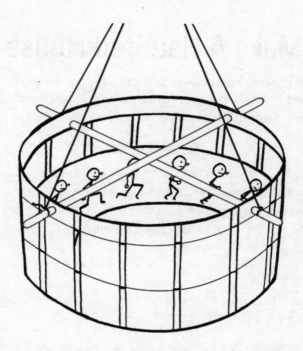

Cut four lengths of string, 50 cm each. Tie a piece to each end of the dowelling rods. Bring the four ends to the middle of the wheel and tie them together.

Suspend the magic wheel by holding the ends of the string in one hand. Now twist the wheel in the opposite direction to the running character. Let go of the wheel and peep through the slats as it spins. Watch as your little figure comes to life! Now spin the wheel in the opposite direction so the character runs backwards and the strings untangle.

Alternative ideas for animations that will work well in your zoetrope are jumping fish and bouncing balls. Keep your sequences simple for the best result.

Make A Haunted House

Get crafting at Halloween and create your very own haunted house – perfect for spooking visitors and great just for a little October fun.

You will need:

- an empty shoe box • white tissue paper
- cotton thread • scissors • a glue stick • sticky tape
- black poster paint • a sizeable lump of modelling clay
- a sharp pencil • a ruler

Cut away one end of the shoe box completely, saving the piece of card for later on.

 Position the opposite end of the box over the piece of modelling clay and use the point of a pencil to make a hole in the middle of the cardboard.

 Paint the inside of the box black and leave it to dry.

Cut out an oblong of tissue paper, slightly larger than the end of the box and tape it over the open end.

Sketch the shape of a bat, a ghost and a cat on the spare piece of card from the end of the shoe box. Cut them out and paint them black. Put them to one side to dry.

When dry, use the point of the pencil to make a hole in the top of each of your scary shapes, pushing through the card into the modelling clay underneath. In the same way, make three holes on each of the long sides of the shoe box in the positions shown.

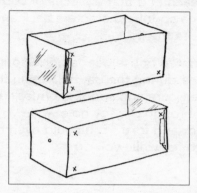

Measure and cut two pieces of cotton that are twice the width of the box and one piece that is twice the length of the box. Thread the longest piece of cotton through the top of the bat and secure with a knot in the centre. Then repeat with the cat and ghost pieces.

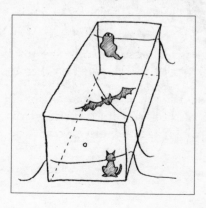

Thread the cat between the two lowest holes at the front of the shoe box and then string the ghost between the two highest holes at the back. Lastly, thread the bat diagonally across the box between the remaining holes.

Tie a loop at each end of the pieces of cotton and use them to pull the spooky characters back and forth inside the box. Replace the lid.

Place your haunted house near a good source of light – a window is fine during the day, a lamp in the evening. Now choose a victim and spook them out, by getting them to look through the spy hole while you pull the characters back and forth. You could even make up scary stories to tell while you do it.

Make A Spectacular Firework Display Picture

Firework displays can be great fun, but it can be tricky to take a really good photograph of the actual fireworks. With these pictures you can get inspiration from your next local display and then come home and make some spectacular displays of your own.

You will need:

- a sheet of paper • colouring pens or pencils
- a large black wax crayon • a pen lid or small coin

- - - - - - - - - - - - - - - - - - - -

Put some sheets of newspaper down to protect the surface you're working on. Now take the coloured pens and start tackling the big, white space of the paper. You want to cover the whole sheet in colour – so get stuck in. Try rainbow stripes, random blobs, connecting squares, or anything you like. Just make sure that every bit of white is covered with all of your favourite colours.

When your paper is covered in colour take your black crayon and scribble over your page until it is all black. Don't hold back, the blacker the better. Remember this is supposed to be the night sky.

When the page is completely covered in black crayon and none of the colours underneath are visible, you're ready to 'draw' your picture.

Use a small coin or the lid of a pen to scratch into the surface of the black crayon and reveal the bright colours beneath. Add swirls, star-bursts and spirals, dots, rocket shapes and sparklers. Spectacular!

The great thing is, if you make a mistake or you get bored of your picture, just grab your black crayon again, cover the picture up and start again.

Marble Madness

People have been playing marbles for centuries – even before your parents were little!

The best known method of 'shooting' a marble is a technique called 'fulking'. Bend your index finger into a U-shape and place the second knuckle on the ground. Rest a marble in the U-shape of the bent index finger. Use your thumb to flick the marble off your finger.

Here are some great marble games.

MONEY MARKSMAN

One player places a marble on a coin. The other players attempt to knock it off. Those who miss lose their marbles. The player who manages it wins the coin!

SPANNERS

One player, the 'placer', shoots a marble along the ground. The second player then shoots a marble, attempting to land it within a hand's span of the first marble. If they are successful, they pocket the first marble and the game begins again, with the winner as the placer. If they miss, more players take turns trying to put a marble within a hand's span of the second shot, pocketing all the marbles if successful.

THREE HOLES

Find a flat area of earth in your garden without any grass. Scoop out three small holes in the ground using a sharp stone, stick or trowel. Players take it in turns to try to land marbles in all three holes, one after the other. If a marble hits another marble and shunts it into a hole, that still counts as 'on-target'.

The first player to hole three marbles in three shots wins.

LAG OUT

Place a marble near a wall. Players take turns bouncing marbles off the wall, trying to hit the placed marble. As players fail, there will be more marbles to hit.

Any player who hits a marble can retrieve their marble and choose one other. Keep playing until someone has won all the marbles or all the marbles are on the ground and nobody has won.

Perfect A Picnic Pan Bagna

Pan Bagna literally means 'bathed bread' as the bread is bathed in dressing so that it absorbs all the delicious flavours from the filling.

Pan Bagna are great because people of all ages can prepare them – so there are no excuses not to get involved. They can be made several hours before you go on a picnic, or even the night before.

There are many variations on the fillings, so you can always experiment, but here are a couple of suggestions for you to try.

TUNA PAN BAGNA

You will need:

- 1 ciabatta loaf or French bread • 3 tbsp French dressing
- fresh basil leaves • 3–4 large tomatoes
- 2 hard-boiled eggs • ½ a 185g can of tuna
- 8 pitted olives • 2 tbsp capers
- 2 spring onions, chopped

- -

Cut the bread lengthways so that only one side is cut through while the other remains attached. (If using a baguette, cut in half first). Slice the tomatoes and eggs and cut the olives in half.

Sprinkle the insides of the bread with the dressing and cover with the fresh basil leaves. Layer the rest of the ingredients on top.

Close the loaf and wrap it tightly in plastic wrap. Then chill it in the fridge for at least two hours. Cut into portions before eating.

PAN BAGNA PROVENÇAL

You will need:

- 1 very large, round, country-style loaf or ciabatta
- 100 g (4 oz) pesto • 120 ml (¼ pint) French dressing
- 150 g (5 oz) salami • 4 large tomatoes, sliced
- 10–20 pitted olives • 8 slices prosciutto ham

- 250 g (9 oz) fresh basil or rocket
- 250 g (9 oz) pepperdew chillies
  or pimentos in syrup, drained

- - - - - - - - - - - - - - - - - - -

If using a round loaf, slice off the top and keep it to serve as a lid. With a ciabatta, slice it lengthways so that only one side is cut through while the other remains attached.

Tear out the bread in the centre of the loaf, leaving a hollow 2 cm deep. Using a food processor, turn the bread into breadcrumbs and then mix half of them with the pesto. Mix the other half with the French dressing.

Add two-thirds of the pesto mix to the bottom half of the bread, then layer the salami, tomato, olives, French dressing mixture, prosciutto, basil or rocket, peppers and then the remainder of the pesto mix. Pack everything in and close the pan bagna.

Tightly wrap in plastic wrap and chill in the fridge. Finally unwrap and slice into portions.

A sharp knife is recommended to divide up the loaves but they can be broken with your hands – it just tends to be a bit messy.

Make Fortune Cookies

Fortune cookies are delicious treats with a surprise inside. They are great fun at parties and can be even more fun if you write your own fortunes to put in them.

You will need:

- 2 egg whites • ½ tsp vanilla extract
- 1 pinch salt • 35 g (1¼ oz) flour
- 50 g (1¾ oz) white sugar
- a sheet of plain paper • a pen/pencil

THE FORTUNES

Before you start to cook, cut the paper into strips of around 7½ cm by 1 cm so they are slim enough to fit inside the cookies.

Write your fortunes. Make them as general as possible as you don't know who will pick which cookie. Never put bad fortunes in as they might be taken seriously.

Traditional messages include, 'You will live long and prosper', or 'Seven will be your lucky number this weekend'.

THE COOKIES

Put the egg whites in a large bowl with the vanilla extract. Whisk until fluffy but not stiff. Add the flour, salt and sugar and mix together.

Place teaspoonfuls of the batter 10 cm apart on a baking sheet and tilt so that they make circles of about 7½ cm in diameter.

Bake for 5 minutes at gas mark 6/200°C/400°F or until the cookies are golden at the edges. In the meantime, prepare the next sheet and put these in the oven when the first batch is ready.

Take the cookies out of the oven and quickly remove them with a wide spatula, placing upside down on a wooden board. Put the fortune onto the cookie, close to the middle, and fold the cookie in half.

Holding the folded cookie in both hands, between your thumb and index fingers, fold in half again so that it is in quarters. If your cookie is a little stiff pull the ends down over the rim of a glass or the handle of a wooden spoon, until the ends meet. The opened side of the fortune cookie should be facing upwards, towards you.

Always use cold baking sheets, as warm ones will make them cook too quickly.

You must work fast with the cookies in the final stages as the cookies set very quickly. For best results do three or four cookies at a time.

Top tip: If you can find a pair of cotton gloves to help you touch the cookies when they are hot, it will help.

How Does Your Miniature Garden Grow?

Miniature gardens are wonderfully versatile. They can provide a handy windowsill kitchen garden, a tropical jungle for a toy T. rex to roam in, or an enchanted fairy kingdom. You could even recreate the Hanging Gardens of Babylon in miniature.

PREPARATION

The beauty of a miniature garden is that it can be created anywhere. You may have a window box or flowerbed you could use, or you may prefer to use a pot or trough so that you can move your garden wherever you like it.

Select your plants. For this you need to decide whether yours is an indoor or an outdoor garden, as this will affect the type of plants that you choose. It is a good idea to ask a member of staff at your local garden centre to help with your selection. They will be able to recommend interesting plants that are suited to your garden's soil and climate. Here are some ideas to get you started.

IDEAS FOR INDOOR PLANTS

- miniature boxwood
- scented miniature cyclamen
- miniature roses • miniature African violets
- herbs (e.g. parsley)

IDEAS FOR OUTDOOR PLANTS

- alpine trees (e.g. Baggesen's Gold) and conifers of the 'Chamaecyparis' variety.
- miniature weeping willow
- miniature jasmine
- miniature grass

PLANNING

Next you need to decide how you are going to arrange your garden. Draw out a garden plan, taking into account the shape of your plot or container. When drawing your plan you should add any features you want to include, such as benches, arches or water features. You should also mark out where you are going to have any gravel paths or stepping stones.

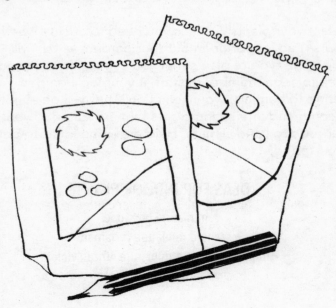

PLANTING

Once you have got your plants and designed your garden, it is time to begin planting.

Place a brick or a flat piece of paving at the bottom of your trough or container. Add some gravel or stones for drainage. Then spread your compost above this about 10 cm deep.

Dig holes in the compost and then carefully remove the plants from their plastic pots. Place the plants in the holes and fill around them with earth, pressing down firmly on the soil. Once all the plants are in place you can add your own decorative features (see the suggestions below).

IDEAS FOR GARDEN FEATURES

- Decking - use small pieces of wood, twigs or lollipop sticks.

- Patio - use small stones and pebbles.

- Mountain ranges - use larger stones.

- Paths - coloured gravel for fish tanks work well and can be bought from garden centres or pet shops.

- Furniture - you may have dolls' house furniture you could use, but be careful in outdoor gardens as it could be damaged by the weather.

- Water features – these can be relaxing places for the tiny inhabitants of your garden or a watering hole for a velociraptor toy. They can be made from a small mirror or a sunken dish filled with water. Float a leaf and a small flower on this and it will look like a beautiful water lily.

- Glass pebbles – you can buy these at most florists. They make magical additions to the landscape.

UPKEEP

Your miniature garden will need regular watering. Make sure you keep the borders neat, and trim any plants that look like they are becoming unruly. New features like birdbaths or statues can be added as and when you find them or whenever you feel like giving the garden a completely new look.

Meet Mr Turf Top

Give an old pair of tights a terrific turf toupée with this fun gardening project that'll keep everyone amused for weeks on end.

You will need:

- old nylon tights
- sawdust • grass seed
- elastic bands • a small saucer
- lips cut from felt or fabric
- eyes made from card or wiggle eyes (available in craft shops) • a pair of scissors

Cut off one leg of the tights and discard the rest. Pour a large spoonful of grass seed into the foot and spread it around the toe area. Stuff the end of the tights with sawdust until the 'head' is the size you want.

Secure at the bottom with an elastic band, or simply tie it in a knot. Make sure that the seed is spread evenly where you want the hair to grow. Then create a nose by pinching a small section of nylon and sawdust and wrapping an elastic band around each one. Glue on eyes and lips.

Lastly, soak Mr Turf Top in a small bowl of water so that the sawdust is damp, then sit him comfortably in the saucer and watch his hair grow.

Don't forget to keep the saucer topped up with a little water every so often and give him an occasional trim.

Indoor And Outdoor Games

Long ago, when your parents were young, they couldn't always play outside because of the sabre-toothed tigers and woolly mammoths that roamed the Earth. Here are some games that are great to play when you are stuck indoors, and one to play when the coast is clear outside.

SARDINES

This game is hide-and-seek in reverse and it is usually played indoors.

One person hides, while everyone else counts to 50 very slowly. To stop people from rattling through the numbers too fast, you must count, 'One-tyrannosaurus, two-diplodocus, three-tyrannosaurus,' all the way to 50.

Then the seekers split up and start hunting. If a seeker finds the person that is hiding, they squash in next to them in the hiding place.

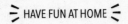

The loser is the last person to find the hiding place where all the other players are squashed together like sardines in a can.

DUCK, DUCK, GOOSE

This is another great indoor game for four players or more. One person is the 'goose' and the other players are 'ducks'. The ducks sit in a circle on the floor while the 'goose' prowls around the circle.

When the goose touches one of the duck's shoulders, that duck has to leap to their feet. Both the duck and the goose sprint round the circle until they return to the empty space. The first person back to the empty space sits down. The person still standing becomes the goose.

FORTY-FORTY

This is an outdoor game. Choose a base, such as a garden tree or bush. One person is picked to be the hunter. The object of the game is to hide while the hunter counts to 40. When the hunter leaves the base to start looking, the hunted need to try to get back to the base without being caught.

The hunter doesn't have to touch the players to catch them out – they just have to see them, then run back to base and shout, 'Forty-forty, I see you!', and name the person that they've seen.

If the hunted can run fast and beat the hunter back to base, they are safe. The last person to be caught is the hunter in the next round.

Build A Pixie House

Everyone who believes in elves and pixies knows that they can't resist visiting a garden or park when there's a secret house waiting. Make a hideaway for tiny folk using a handful of natural materials and just a sprinkling of your imagination.

You will need:

- a small bundle of sticks about 15 cm long
- some string, ribbon or grass • a thimble or acorn shell
- soft moss • feathers or flower heads • small stones

Find a secluded spot in your garden or a nearby park. You will need a small area measuring about 15 cm by 15 cm, away from noisy footsteps. The foot of a tree or behind a bush is perfect, as this will provide your fairy folk with some welcome privacy.

Ideally your chosen spot will have moist soil. This will make your house easier to build. If the soil is dry and hard try sprinkling some water over it.

Collect a small bundle of sticks that are about 15 cm long. Snap longer twigs to this size if necessary, but be sure not to break any twigs or branches off living trees.

Push the sticks about 2 cm into the ground to form a circle shape about 15 cm in diameter. The sticks should point inwards slightly so that they form a cone-shape, like a teepee. Leave a gap in the circle about 4 cm wide for the door, so pixies can tiptoe inside.

Tie the string or ribbon around the top of the twigs to bind them tightly together. It will be easier if one of you holds the twigs together while the other ties them.

Use blades of grass to tie feathers or flowers around the top of the house to make it look more welcoming. Carpet the floor with a layer of luxurious soft moss and place a ring of stones around the edge of the house to protect it from nosy animals. Build a path of stepping-stones leading up to the house using small stones or pebbles to lead the pixies to the door.

Finally, place a thimble, or an acorn shell filled with water, inside the house to welcome thirsty travellers.

Elves and pixies are very shy and so won't use the house until you are well out of the way.

Make A Swirler Whirler

In the 18th century, before computer games were even invented, this simple toy kept people occupied for hours. What are you waiting for? Give it a whirl.

You will need:

- stiff white card • colouring pens
- elastic thread (about 60 cm long)
- a large jam jar lid • scissors

Place the jam jar lid on the card. Draw around it twice to make two separate circles and cut them out.

Decorate one side of each circle with bold patterns. You could divide one of them into different coloured quarters and the other into coloured stripes.

With the tip of a pair of scissors, gently poke two small holes in each circle about 1 cm either side of the central point. The holes should be just big enough to thread the elastic thread through.

Place the two circles, plain sides together.

Then thread the elastic one way through both circles, loop around, then pass one way back through both circles. Tie the two ends of the elastic together.

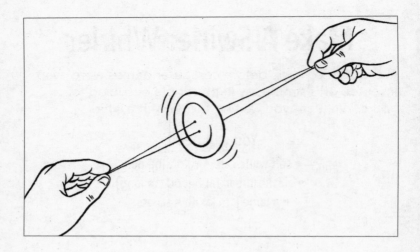

Tuck your middle fingers through each loop of elastic. Then, using your thumbs and index fingers, twist the disks so they rotate away from you, over and over, until the elastic is taut. This can be awkward, but you will soon get the knack.

Finally, pull both loops outwards, so that the elastic untwists and the disks spin. Maintain the spin by moving your hands in and out – increasing and decreasing the tension on the elastic. Watch as the patterns you have drawn distort.

You can experiment by drawing different patterns on the disks to see what they look like when they swirl. Try hearts, spots, stars and zigzags.

Make Chocolate Leaves

Chocolate leaves make impressive and delicious decorations for cakes or desserts.

You will need:

- 115 g plain chocolate
- non-toxic leaves such as rose, lemon or bay leaves
- a pastry brush
- greaseproof paper

Carefully wash the leaves and pat them dry using a clean tea towel.

Cover your work surface with a sheet of newspaper to protect it from any stray dribbles of chocolate, and lay some greaseproof paper on a tray ready for your leaves.

Break the chocolate into chunks in a glass bowl.

 Melt the chocolate either on low power in the microwave, or over a pan of boiling water, stirring until it is runny.

When the chocolate has melted, remove it from the heat. Use a table knife or pastry brush to spread a thick and even layer of chocolate on the underside (the bumpy side) of each leaf. Take care not to go over the edges or your leaves will be difficult to peel off later.

Place the leaves, chocolate side up, on the tray lined with greaseproof paper or over a rolling pin to give them a nice curl. Put them in the fridge for about an hour.

Take the leaves out of the fridge. Holding the stalk, gently peel the leaf away from the chocolate. Don't worry if some of your leaves break at this stage. With patience and practice you will have forests of them!

Refrigerate the chocolate leaves in an airtight container until you can resist them no longer.

Have A Bubble Party

Why not have a bubble-blowing competition – the bigger the bubbles the better? Here are some tips on how to make the best bubbles ever.

THE PERFECT MIX

For a great bubble mixture, add eight tablespoons of washing up liquid and four tablespoons of glycerin (available from any pharmacist) to a litre of water. Leave the mixture to stand overnight.

For extra effect, add a few drops of food-colouring into the mix – but head outside if you do this, as things could gets messy!

A GIANT BUBBLE MAKER

Pour your bubble mix into a large, shallow tray. Thread two straws onto a metre length of string. Tie the string in a loop between the two straws.

Holding a straw in each hand as handles, dip the loop into your bubble mix, then gently lift it out. You should have a shimmering film of bubble mix in the middle of your loop.

Hold one arm above the other and spin your whole body around in a slow circle. The mixture in the loop should billow out into a bubble.

Try twisting the straws to bring the two sides of the loop together, allowing the bubble to float free.

Top tip: As you get better at this bubble-making method, increase the length of the string – see if a parent could manage a piece 3 m long.

Compete to see who can make the biggest bubble, who can make a bubble last the longest and who can catch a bubble without bursting it.

BUBBLE PIPE

To make a bubble pipe, use the tip of a ballpoint pen to make a small hole near the base of a polystyrene cup.

Insert the short end of a bendy straw into the hole and point the end up towards the top of the cup.

Fill the cup with enough bubble mix to cover the tip of the straw. Holding the other end of the straw level with the top of the cup, blow gently into the straw and the liquid will start to foam and bubble.

Haircare At Home

AVOCADO HAIR PACK

Avocados are packed with vitamins and can give your hair a real treat, rehydrating it and leaving it feeling smooth and looking shiny.

You will need:

- 1 small jar of mayonnaise (not the low-fat type!)
- ½ a ripe avocado • shower cap or plastic wrap

Put the ingredients into a bowl and, using your hands or a spoon, squash the avocado into the mayonnaise until it forms a green paste.

Smooth over the hair, from the roots to the tips. Put on a shower cap (the ones they give you at hotels are ideal for this) or wrap the hair in plastic wrap.

For hair in need of extra deep conditioning, wrap a hot, damp towel over the top of the cap or wrap. This may need two pairs of hands.

Wait for 20 minutes before rinsing with lots of clean, warm water.

LAVENDER HAIR RINSE

This not only smells lovely, but lavender is thought to be a natural remedy for dandruff. Pour half a cup of dried lavender into a pan, with two cups of water. Bring to the boil and simmer for 3 minutes then allow the mixture to cool. Use the lavender water as a hair conditioner after washing your hair and leave it on for 15 minutes before rinsing off with water.

ROSEMARY RINSE

Boil a large saucepan of water, then take a bunch of fresh rosemary and add it to the pan. Simmer for half an hour and leave to cool before straining.

This should only be used on dark hair as it can darken blonde hair. It adds shine, helps itchy scalps, and smells really great.

Make A Super Scrunchie

Use your brand new sewing skills learned on pages 37 to 39 to make a fabulous hair accessory. Making your own accessories means you can match them exactly to your outfit. Scrunchies are great to make as gifts or to sell at the school fête.

You will need:

- fabric measuring 42 cm x 13 cm
- elastic – width ½ cm, length 26 cm
- 2 safety pins • needle and thread

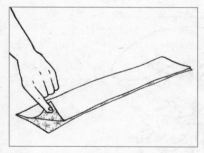

Fold the fabric over along the long side, so that only the underside shows.

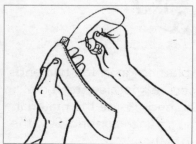

Using backstitch (see page 38) sew along the open edge about 2 cm in. Turn the fabric tube right side out.

Pin one of the safety pins to the end of the elastic and attach it to one end of the tube.

Pin the other pin to the opposite end of the elastic and thread the elastic through the tube.

Undo the safety pins, without letting go of the two ends of the elastic and then tie a secure knot, leaving 5 cm of elastic at the ends. Tuck the ends inside the material. Fold over the cut edges of the scrunchie fabric. Sew the two ends of the fabric tube together.

Build A Water Obstacle Course

You need steady hands and a quick brain to race around an obstacle course carrying a brimming beaker of water.

This is an outdoor game, unless you want to turn your lounge into a swimming pool. You don't need a big space to play it, just a big imagination.

HOW TO PLAY

The race starts at a paddling pool full of water, or a tap, and ends with a row of buckets, one for each player.

Each contestant holds a plastic beaker of water and races around an obstacle course before emptying the water into the bucket. This is repeated ten times. The winner is the player with the most water in their bucket at the end.

To avoid any confusion over whose bucket is whose, label each one with a contestant's name.

THE OBSTACLES

Hunt around your home and garden for objects that can be turned into obstacles. Try some of these challenges and experiment by building your own obstacles and inventing your own moves. (Don't forget to take a beaker of water with you.)

- Walk backwards around the paddling pool.

- Run around a deckchair three times.

- Walk along a plank balanced on bricks.

- Hop back and forth over a bamboo cane four times.

- Do three keepie-uppies with a football (see page 24).

- Add in a star-jump.

- If you are feeling brave and don't mind getting drenched, balance the beaker on your head for three seconds.

Top tips: Make the challenge even harder by not allowing racers to cover their beakers with their hands.

To even up the challenge, give younger players a bigger beaker or a saucepan. Or instead of a bucket, give them an ice cream tub to fill at the end.

Harness Balloon Power

Have your parents got enough puff or patience to make a jet-powered toy using a party balloon?

MAKE A MINI JET BOAT

Who needs a real-life speed boat, when you can create a miniature version to race in your bath?

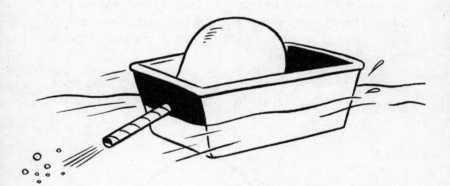

You will need:

- a large margarine tub • a balloon
- the barrel of a ballpoint pen • an elastic band
- a lump of modelling clay • scissors

- - - - - - - - - - - - - - - - - -

Start by placing a lump of modelling clay in one end of the margarine tub. This will ensure the boat sits deep in the water instead of bobbing on top.

With the scissors, pierce the end of the tub (the one that is closest to the lump of clay) near the base. Make a hole just big enough to poke the plastic pen barrel through.

Slip the pen barrel through the hole you have made in the tub and into the neck of the balloon. Seal the hole around the pen with more modelling clay. The balloon will be resting inside your tub. Secure it by wrapping the elastic band round and round.

Blow through the pen barrel to inflate the balloon. This takes a lot of puff! When you are finished blowing, hold your finger over the hole at the end of the barrel to stop the air from escaping.

Now put the speedboat in a bathtub or paddling pool and remove your thumb from the hole to set it racing.

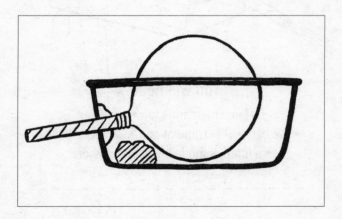

Top tip: Why not make a boat with someone else and see whose boat sails for the longest amount of time? You could even try racing them.

Seriously Super Smoothies

A smoothie will provide goodness for your insides as well as tasting great. Shop-bought smoothies are usually expensive, but this quick, simple drink is far cheaper and is made with fresh, natural ingredients packed with healthy vitamins.

You will need:

- 1 small tub of fruit yogurt • 1 glass of milk
- 1 ripe banana • a handful of soft fruit (strawberries, raspberries and blackberries work particularly well)

Slice the banana and put into a blender or liquidizer. Add the yogurt and fruit and blend for a minute. Add the milk and blend for a few seconds more. Pour and enjoy!

Make The Perfect Omelette

Omelettes are the original fast food and can provide a filling, nutritious meal in minutes. Simple as they seem, it's easy to make them too stodgy or too thin.

You will need:

- 3 eggs
- a pinch of mixed herbs
- a knob of butter
- a 20 cm frying pan (15 cm for a two-egg omelette)
- salt and pepper

- - - - - - - - - - - - - - - - - - -

Break the eggs into a bowl, add the salt, pepper and herbs and then beat the egg mixture lightly with a fork.

 Place the pan over a medium heat. Add the butter and then tilt the pan over the heat so that the melting butter coats the bottom.

Turn up the heat and pour in the beaten eggs.

Allow the mixture to set a little and then use a spatula to push it away from the sides. Tip the pan so that any uncooked egg on top runs to the edges. When the top is almost cooked, take the spatula and fold the omelette in half. Tip it on to a warm plate and serve immediately.

Top tip: Once you have mastered the perfect omelette, experiment with different fillings. Any of the following ingredients can be added to the egg mixture:

- chopped ham • chopped cooked bacon • grated cheese – approximately 25 g (1 oz) per egg • chopped tomatoes
- potatoes, pre-cooked and chopped

Top tip: The key to a light, fluffy omelette is making sure the butter is hot before you add the eggs and always using the right-sized pan.

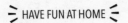
Make Paper Helicopters

Imagine having your very own helicopter that is easy to land and does not have any complicated controls. See who can make the best helicopter that spins the fastest.

WHIRLY BIRD

To make one, cut a strip of paper 3 cm by 12 cm. Make a cut, a centimetre deep, at the midpoint of each long side.

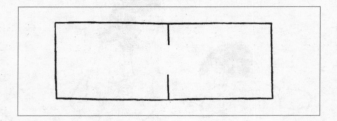

Now score a line from the bottom of each cut along the left-hand side of the cut to the edge of the paper.

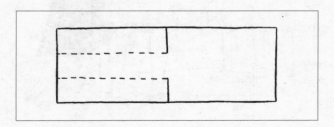

Fold the bottom section up along the score line and then fold the top section down as shown below.

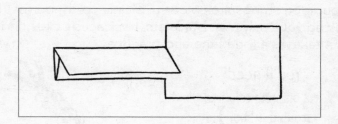

Now the left-hand side of the strip is three-times thicker and 1 cm wide. Slip a paperclip over the end.

Make a 4 cm cut along the middle of the right-hand half. Fold the lower piece down flat. Turn the paper over and turn the other half of the strip down.

Pick up the paper and straighten out the two wider pieces, to make a T-shape.

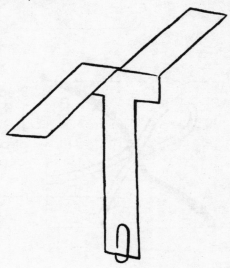

Hold the helicopter by the paperclipped leg above your head and let it go. Watch those blades whirl!

Top tip: Try adding more paperclips to make your helicopter spin and fall faster.

Knot A Scoubidou Key Ring

Scoubidou strings are colourful plastic cords, perfect for making your very own bracelets, necklaces or key rings. All it takes is a little time and practice.

You'll need:

- 2 different-coloured scoubidou strands
- a split ring that takes keys
- a medium-sized bead (match it with your scoubidou colours, if you can)

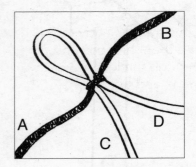

Step 1. Make a small loop in the middle of one strand and then tie the different coloured strand around the loop in a knot. This will be the loop you attach the split ring to.

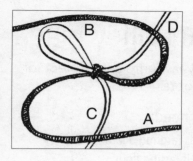

Step 2. You now have four scoubidou strands, A and B in one colour, C and D in a second colour. Arrange the colours so that they are opposite each other in a cross.

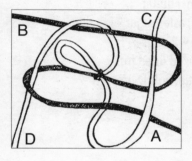

Step 3. Make a loop in strand A and a loop in strand B as shown. Now thread strand C through loop A and strand D through loop B and pull tight. The knot should now look like a chequered square.

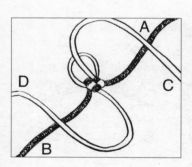

Step 4. Repeat step three, but this time make loops with strand C and strand D and then thread A and B through the loops you have made and tighten.

Continue your scoubidou, alternating the knots made in steps 3 and 4 until it is as long as you want. Leave a 6 cm length at the end of each strand. To add a bead, thread your bead over all four strands before making a final knot.

Banana Loaf

A banana loaf is a huge family favourite and perfect for any picnic, or a day spent indoors.

You will need:

- 450 g (1 lb) soft bananas (around 3 large ones)
- 225 g (8 oz) self-raising flour
- 100 g (4 oz) butter
- 150 g (5 oz) caster sugar
- ½ tsp salt • 2 eggs
- 225 g (8 oz) mixed dried fruit
- a 900 g (2 lb) loaf tin, lightly greased

Preheat the oven to gas mark 4/180°C/350°F.

 While the oven is warming up, peel the bananas and mash them with a fork in a large bowl.

Add the rest of the ingredients, except for the dried fruit. Mix until thoroughly blended, then add the dried fruit and mix again.

Pour the mixture into your loaf tin and bake in the oven for 1½ hours.

 You can tell if the loaf is properly cooked by pushing a metal skewer or knife into the middle of it. If it comes out clean, your banana loaf is done.

Cool on a wire rack.

Breathtaking Ball Spinning

Find out who can master this brilliant ball trick first, and who can achieve the longest spin.

Place the ball on your upturned palm, with your arm extended and slightly bent at the elbow. Practise flicking the ball about 6 cm into the air with a pat of your hand. Try putting some spin on the ball by rotating your wrist with an anti-clockwise flick if you are right-handed. (If you are left-handed, rotate your wrist clockwise.)

When you can do this confidently, as the ball leaves your hand, point your index finger up and let the ball land directly onto it. (Practise so you make contact at the centre of the ball.) The more spin you put on the ball as it goes up, the faster and longer it will spin.

If you're getting really good, try flicking it up from your fingertip to increase the spin and catching it again. Do this correctly and the ball will look like it's weightless.

Fresh Pasta Feast

This recipe makes delicious fresh tagliatelle for four people – perfect to serve up with Mama's Meatballs (See page 184).

You will need:

• 200 g (7 oz) plain flour • 2 eggs • a pinch of salt

Combine the flour and salt in a large bowl. Crack the eggs into another bowl and beat lightly with a fork. Make a well in the middle of the flour and pour in the beaten eggs. Stir together until firm. At this stage, if your dough feels dry, add a little water – if it seems sticky, add some extra flour.

Place the dough onto a floured surface and knead thoroughly for 10 minutes until smooth and shiny. Cover in plastic wrap and leave to rest for 15 minutes.

Unwrap the dough and roll it out on a floured surface into a long rectangle shape about 1 mm thick. Dust the pasta sheet with flour to prevent sticking and carefully fold the narrow edge of the sheet over by 4 cm. Continue folding until the whole sheet is rolled up into a long tube.

Take a knife and cut strips of pasta 1 cm wide from the folded piece until you reach the end. Unfold the strips and leave to dry for a few minutes before cooking.

Cook the pasta in boiling water for 4 to 5 minutes, tasting a piece to see if it is ready. Drain and serve.

Mama's Meatballs

This has long been a staple dish in parts of southern Italy and, as many Italian-Americans hail from this region, it has become a firm family-favourite in the US, too.

You will need:

- 2 slices of white bread
- 100 g (4 oz) Parmesan cheese, grated
- 400 g (14 oz) lean minced beef
- 1 tbsp fresh parsley, chopped • 2 eggs
- 1 tbsp olive oil • 1 onion, finely chopped
- 2 x 400 g (14 oz) cans chopped tomatoes
- salt and pepper • 400 g (14 oz) dried spaghetti

This recipe will feed four to five hungry people.

 Using a food processor, whizz the bread into fine crumbs. If you don't have a food processor, break the bread into crumbs in a bowl. Add the parsley and half of the Parmesan cheese and stir together. Add the mince and a good grind of freshly milled black pepper.

Break the eggs into the bowl and mix. Squash the mixture together with your hands until it is thoroughly blended.

Roll the mixture into balls the size of a large walnut and place on a baking tray covered in plastic wrap. Put to one side for later.

Heat the olive oil in a large saucepan and fry the onion until soft. Add the tomatoes and some salt and pepper. Bring to the boil and then turn down the heat to simmer for ten minutes. Drop in the meatballs one by one and then cover the pan. Simmer for one hour.

After about 40 minutes cook the spaghetti according to the instructions on the pack or cook your fresh tagliatelle (see page 183). Drain the pasta and turn into a serving dish. Stir in the cooked meatballs and remaining cheese. Serve immediately.

Top tip: If you prefer a sweeter sauce, add a ½ tsp of sugar to your sauce before you add the meatballs.

Fairground Fun

Roll up, roll up and enjoy your very own fairground attraction. See who has the best aim when taking a pot shot!

You will need:

- 4 empty six-packs of yogurts
(each of the pots must be big enough to fit a ping-pong ball and make sure the pots are still joined together)
- a large cardboard box measuring
at least 30 cm by 45 cm • five ping-pong balls
- coloured acrylic paints • scissors • glue • masking tape

- - - - - - - - - - - - - - - - - - -

Tape the four yogurt six-packs into a rectangle (as shown in the picture). These are your targets.

Paint the top of each six-pack a different colour. Devise your own scoring system by painting a number between one and ten next to each hole. Leave the pots to dry.

Meanwhile, cut off the front and top of the cardboard box. Glue the bottoms of the yogurt pots inside the cardboard box.

To make your target board tilt towards you, put a couple of books under the end of the box.

Stand at a specified distance from your target board (younger players can be a little closer than others) and take turns in seeing who can score the highest number of points by throwing five ping-pong balls.

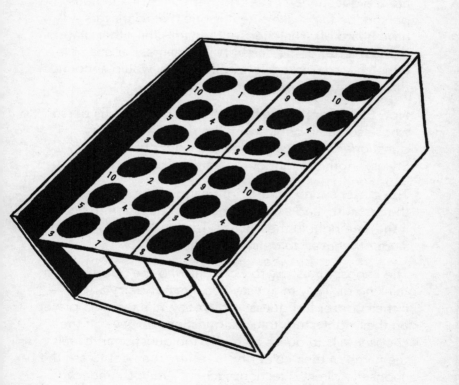

Your Five Minutes Of Fame

Why not play a great game called 'Botticelli'? It is perfect for two or more players and will bring a touch of star quality to boring days stuck at home.

For each round, one person is the chooser and the rest are the questioners. The chooser thinks of a famous person (be fair, make sure it is one that all players will have heard of). The chooser then tells the other players the first letter of the celebrity's surname. For example, if the chooser picked Taylor Swift, they would announce that the surname began with the letter 'S'.

Now the other players have to think of a famous person whose surname begins with the right letter. One questioner might guess that the celebrity was Harry Styles, another might guess Steven Spielberg.

The player sitting on the right hand of the chooser takes the first turn, and asks the chooser a question to find out if they are right in their guess. They might ask *'Are you a singer that used to be in a boyband?'*

The chooser must try to work out who the questioner is thinking of. They might say *'No, I'm not Harry Styles.'* If the chooser has guessed correctly, it is the next player on their right's turn to ask a question. However, if the chooser fails to guess correctly, the questioner reveals the name of their celebrity. In return, they get to ask the chooser a direct question, such as *'Are you American?'* The chooser can only answer *'yes'* or *'no'*.

Each time the answer is *'yes'*, the guesser is allowed to ask another question, until they can guess the identity

of the celebrity or until they ask a question that receives the answer 'no'.

If a guesser thinks they know the identity of the chooser's celebrity they must ask a question – for example, 'Are you Taylor Swift?'

The person who guesses correctly is the chooser in the next round.

WHY BOTTICELLI?

This game is named after Sandro Botticelli because, as a rule of thumb, the stars that players choose should never be more obscure than him. You may well ask – who was Sandro Botticelli? Well, he was an Italian painter, but this demonstrates that choosers should only pick well-known celebrities about whom they know something.

The 'If You Really Had To Choose' Game

This is a great game that should spark some very interesting and bizarre conversations, and the best thing about it is that it can be played anywhere.

Each player takes it in turns to present the other players with an imaginary scenario. The scenario has two possible outcomes, which players have to choose between. Players can't say 'neither' or 'both'.

The scenarios can be as crazy and unrealistic as you like – the quirkier, the better.

For example:

If you really had to choose one of these animals as a pet, would you rather have a man-eating tiger or a crocodile?

If you really had to choose, would you prefer your left arm to be made from jelly or cake?

It you really had to choose, would you rather sit in a bath filled with maggots or eat worms?

This game works best if you make your options really difficult to choose between. They could be really yucky, really yummy, really scary, or really funny. This is a fantastic way to find out more about each other, and there are no winners or losers. So what are you waiting for? Get those brain-boggling questions ready!

First published in Great Britain in 2020 by Buster Books,
an imprint of Michael O'Mara Books Limited,
9 Lion Yard, Tremadoc Road, London SW4 7NQ

W www.mombooks.com/buster

f Buster Books

y @BusterBooks

Copyright © Buster Books 2020

Material taken from:

Things to Do with Dad © Michael O'Mara Books Limited 2008
Things to Do with Mum © Michael O'Mara Books Limited 2008

Illustrations copyright © Karen Donnelly 2008
Illustrations copyright © A.J. Garces 2008

A CIP catalogue record for this book is available from the British Library.

ISBN: 978-1-78055-736-6

2 4 6 8 10 9 7 5 3 1

Papers used by Buster Books are natural, recyclable products made of wood
from well-managed, FSC®-certified forests and other controlled sources.
The manufacturing processes conform to the environmental regulations
of the country of origin.

Printed and bound in May 2020 by CPI Group (UK) Ltd,
108 Beddington Lane, Croydon, CR0 4YY, United Kingdom

MIX
Paper from
responsible sources
FSC® C020471